**W9-CEF-085**

EX LIBRIS

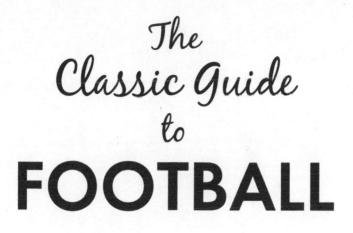

# The
# Classic Guide
# to
# FOOTBALL

# The
# Classic Guide
# to
# FOOTBALL

## C. W. ALCOCK

AMBERLEY

Originally published in 1906
This edition first published 2014

Amberley Publishing
The Hill, Stroud, Gloucestershire, GL5 4EP
www.amberley-books.com

ISBN 978 1 4456 4016 7 (print)
ISBN 978 1 4456 4026 6 (ebook)

British Library Cataloguing in Publication Data.
A catalogue record for this book is available from the British Library.

Typesetting by Amberley Publishing.
Printed in Great Britain.

# Contents

C. W. Alcock.

# Introduction

The beautiful game as we know it today originated at the end of the nineteenth century. While the history of football as a sport in England can be traced back to at least the eighth century – outside of the UK it goes back to Ancient Greece – the laws of the modern game were first standardised between 1848, when the Cambridge Rules were drawn up at Trinity College in a meeting attended by representatives from Eton, Harrow, Rugby, Winchester and Shrewsbury schools; 1858, when the Sheffield rules were adopted by several Midlands and Northern clubs; and 1877, when full unity of the Sheffield rules was established. The formation of the Football Association in 1863 only strengthened football as an institution, and the split with Rugby football in 1871 finally gave Association football its own, very distinct, identity. The International Football Association Board was formed in 1886 to determine and maintain the laws of the game. Two years later, the world's first Football League was formed in Birmingham by Aston Villa director William McGregor.

Today, football is a multi-billion pound industry, played at professional level all over the world and watched by millions of people. At the time of writing, in 2014, the centenary of both the Football League's founding and the 150th anniversary of the birth of the FA have just passed, and the England national football team is about to enter its fourteenth FIFA World Cup. What more opportune time to take a look at the early history of soccer, and take advice on tactics and training from one of the game's pioneers.

Charles William Alcock has been described as one of the founding fathers of the modern game. He was one of those responsible for the first international football match against Scotland. In 1871, in his position as Secretary to the Football Association, he founded the world's oldest footballing competition, the FA Cup. As a player, he formed the Forest club, and later their more famous successor, Wanderers FC, in 1863. He played at centre-forward, and was known for his accuracy. He later captained England in a match *v.* Scotland, scoring once in a 2-2 draw. Later, as noted, he was FA Secretary from 1870 to 1895, and later became Vice President. He refereed in several FA Cup finals, and also compiled the *Football Annual*.

Aside from his professional qualifications, Alcock was also one of the pioneers of the modern game, and made many reforms that led to a more 'scientific' method of play. He was the first player to be ruled offside in 1866, while probing the ways in which this rule might be exploited, and he was one of the first players to be described as showing teamwork tactics during games. Then, in 1874, he was the first to lend his support to the style of passing that later evolved into the Combination game.

Alcock died in 1907, aged sixty-four. He lived in a time of revolution for football, which, it could be argued, has led to the great success and popularity of the game today. As a journalist, he set down much of the history and knowledge he had accumulated over his long career in one of the very first 'manuals' of the sport in 1906 – *Football: The Association Game*. *The Classic Guide to Football* is a remastered version of this seminal work and includes many contemporary illustrations.

*The Editor*

# 1

# The Formation of the Association

Any treatise on latter-day football would be incomplete without a sketch of the events that led to the formation of the Football Association. The modern revival of football, indeed, practically dates from the inception of that organisation, the largest of the many societies that now direct the forces of football. The institution of the Association, as a matter of fact, marked the first attempt to bring the many different sects into which football players were then divided under the control of one central body. Forty years ago, there was little or no football outside the public schools. In some of them it still lingered, the survival, in a modified form of course, of the rough and semi-barbarous sport of the last century. Even in the majority of these, though, it only occupied a comparatively inferior position, regarded merely as a part of the curriculum of physical training. An occasional visit of a team of Old Boys would arouse a little excitement, but only of a transient character, and with the arrival of spring the schoolboy's fancy would lightly turn to thought of other games. What was worse too, in many cases the schools had special codes of their own. Every one did what was right in his own eyes, and the consequence was a number of games widely different in character, and some of them so divergent as to present, according to outward appearance, no real basis of agreement.

It was to assimilate these conflicting elements, and to harmonise them under the influence of a common set of laws, that the Association first saw the light. At the outset, too, its success seemed to be well assured. At a meeting held at the Freemasons Tavern on 26 October 1863, the Association was formally instituted by a resolution to the effect 'that the clubs represented at this meeting now form themselves into an Association, to be called The Football Association'. The names of those who were present show that there was then at least an honest desire on the part of all who were concerned to prepare a code of rules that would unite all football players under one common and reliable head. The NNs of Kilburn were represented by Mr Arthur Pember, who was subsequently elected the first President of the Association; Barnes, by Mr E. C. Morley, who was for the first few years Hon. Secretary; the War Office Football Club sent Mr E. Wawn; the Crusaders, Mr H. T. Steward; the Forest club, Leytonstone, Mr J. F. Alcock; the Crystal Palace club, Mr F. Day. The Rugby clubs, too, were hardly in a minority as Blackheath, Kensington School, Surbiton, Blackheath Proprietary School, Percival House (Blackheath) each sent a delegate. So far everything augured favourably for the formation of a body that would secure the adhesion of football players of every sect. The first election of officers, too, was conducted in a broad spirit. Mr Arthur Pember, of the NNs, who had taken a prominent part in the organisation, as well as in the successful conduct of the inaugural meeting, was, as already stated, appointed the first President Mr E. C. Morley, of the Barnes club, also well known on the Thames side as an amateur oarsman, another supporter of what I may term, for purposes of distinction, the dribbling game, had the distinction of being chosen the first Hon. Secretary; while the adherents of the Rugby game also had a share in the original management in the selection of Mr G. Campbell, of the Blackheath club, to the post of Treasurer.

Constituted as the meeting was with a fair representation of both sides of football opinion, it is not to be wondered that the initial stages of the movement for federation were marked by a certain amount of harmony. At that time, Eton, Winchester, Westminster, Harrow, Rugby, and Charterhouse were recognised as the leading schools, and, with a view to amalgamate, if possible, their six codes into one uniform set of rules, the Hon. Secretary was instructed to procure the opinions of the different captains on the best means of adapting the various games to admit a code that would be generally satisfactory. At the same time, as the result of a lengthy discussion, on 10 November, it was resolved that the Hon. Secretary should draw up rules to be submitted to a subsequent meeting on the following lines:

1. The length of the ground should not exceed 200 yards.
2. The width of the ground should not exceed 100 yards.
3. The goals should be defined by two upright posts, without any tape or bar across the top of them.
4. That a goal should be scored whenever the ball was kicked between the goalposts or over the spaces between them. That the goalposts be 8 yards apart.
5. That the game be commenced by a place kick from the centre of the ground.

6. The losing side should be entitled to the kick-off.
7. The goals should be changed after each goal is won.
8. That when the ball is out of bounds it should be kicked or thrown in straight by the person who should first touch it down.

The discussion of the proposed laws was resumed a week later, and it was resolved that in addition to the amended rules being drawn up at the last meeting, the Hon. Secretary should draw up rules to be submitted to a subsequent meeting, to the effect that

9. A player is 'out of play' immediately he is in front of the ball, and must return behind the ball as soon as possible. If the ball is kicked by his own side past a player, he may not touch or kick it, or advance until one of the other side has first kicked it, or one of his own side on a level with or in front of him has been able to kick it.

10. In case the ball goes behind the goal line. If the side to whom the goal belongs touches the ball down, one of that side to be entitled to a free-kick from the goal line opposite the place where the ball is touched down. If touched down by one of the opposite side, one of such side shall be entitled to a free-kick (place or drop) from a point fifteen yards outside the goal line opposite the place where the ball is touched down.

11. A player is to be entitled to run with the ball in his hands if he makes a fair catch, or catches the ball on the first bound.

12. A player may be hacked on the front of the leg below the knee while running with the ball.

13. Tripping shall not be allowed except when running with the ball.

14. A player may be held when running with the ball.

15. Hands shall not be used against an adversary except when he is running with the ball.

16. A fair catch is to be when the ball is caught coming directly off an adversary's foot or body. A catch from behind goal or out of touch is not a fair catch.

17. Any player is to be allowed to charge another, provided they are both in active play.

18. No one wearing projecting nails, iron plates, or gutta-percha on the soles or heels of his boots be allowed to play.

19. A player may pass the ball to another player if he makes a fair catch or takes the ball on the first bound.

20. A knock-on is from the hand only.

21. A fair catch is to entitle a player to a free-kick, provided he makes a mark with his heel at once, and in order to take such kick, the player may go as far back as he pleases.

22. A goal is to be scored when the ball passes over the space between the goalposts at whatever height, not being thrown, knocked on, or carried.

A glance at this experimental code will show, as I have already said, that there was, at the inception of the Association, an honest intention on both sides to secure, if possible, a fusion of the two games in the general interest of the game. The chief provisions of the rules in force at Rugby were inserted with a view to a probable compromise. The goal was that in use at Harrow, without any crossbar; but there was a clause to admit of a free-kick (place or drop) in the event of a touchdown by the attacking side, as well as one to allow a fair catch. Further than this, running with the ball in the case of a fair catch or on the first bound was allowed, and even the worst features of the Rugby game, hacking and tripping when running with the ball, were duly provided for.

Looking back by the light of subsequent experience, it seems a pity that the spirit of mutual concession that marked the first stage of the negotiations between the fathers of the Association and Rugby games should not have been maintained until the conferences were brought to a satisfactory issue. It is difficult, though, at the same time, I am bound to confess, to see what compromise could have been effected that would have ensured an amalgamation of rules so utterly dissimilar in their main principles, with one difference at least that seemed likely to prove an obstacle to anything like a permanent settlement

In the meantime, while the leaders of the two great sects into which football players were practically divided were seeking, and earnestly, a basis for mutual agreement, representatives of the principal schools had met at Cambridge with a similar object, to arrange rules which should unite them all under one common head. Of the committee appointed to draw up these rules, the Revd R. Burn, of Shrewsbury School, was the chairman. Eton was represented by Messrs R. H. Blake-Humfrey and W. F. Trench; Rugby, by Messrs W. R. Collyer and M. F. Martin; Harrow, by Messrs J. F. Prior and H. R. Williams; Marlborough, by Mr W. P. Crawley; and Westminster, by Mr W. S. Wright. In these rules a player touching the ball down behind the opposite line was allowed a free-kick twenty-five yards straight out from the goal line. There was no mention, though, of running with the ball, and though there was a stipulation allowing charging, holding, pushing with the hands, tripping up, and running were strictly forbidden. It was, in reality, this Cambridge code that proved to be the rock on which the supporters of the two games split. Still, before this it had been growing more and more apparent that there was little or no possibility of a fusion of the two conflicting interests. It was not until the meeting of the Association, held on 24 November 1863, however, that the irreconcilables came to an actual rupture. A proposal 'that the rules of the Cambridge University embrace the true principles of the game with the greatest simplicity, and, therefore, that a committee be appointed to enter into communication with the committee of the University, to endeavour to induce them to modify some of the rules which appear to the Association to be too lax and liable to give rise to disputes' was declared to be carried in preference to an amendment proposed by Mr Campbell on behalf of the Blackheath club, merely asserting that the Cambridge rules were 'worthy of consideration'. The rejection of this amendment was the first step in the ultimate severance of the two parties upholding respectively the dribbling and the running games. It was not, though, until a fortnight later that the formal withdrawal of the Blackheath club destroyed finally the last hope of a fusion of the rival interests.

Meanwhile, at a meeting held on 1 December, an objection was lodged by the representative of Blackheath to the confirmation of the previous minutes, on the ground that the chairman had taken the votes in favour of the amendment referred to above, and not those against it, so that the record of the meeting was not correct. The minutes, though, were confirmed, with the reservation in the shape of a formal protest from the Blackheath division.

The question of 'hacking' was the rock on which the two parties struck. A proposition that the committee do insist on hacking in their communication with Cambridge had been carried by a bare majority of one vote, only to be reversed in a subsequent conference.

The discussion at this same meeting of 1 December 1863, furnishes such strange reading by the light of public opinion at the present time, that it will be of interest to recapitulate some of the arguments that were adduced on the subject of hacking – pro and con. The rules which practically caused the disruption between the two sections were as follows:

9.   A player shall be entitled to run with the ball towards his adversaries' goal if he makes a fair catch, or catches the ball on the first bound; but in the case of a fair catch, if he makes his mark, he shall not then run.

10.  If any player shall run with the ball towards his adversaries' goal, any player

> on the opposite side shall be at liberty to
> charge, hold, trip, or hack him, or wrest
> the ball from him; but no player shall be
> held and hacked at the same time.

Here was, in fact, the cause of the disagreement.
The Sheffield club, the earliest organisation as far as
I can find for the development of football, had just
given in to its adhesion to the Association. At the
same time, in offering its opinion on the new code,
it expressed its disapproval of the rules just given,
especially of the second, which it declared to be
more suggestive of wrestling. The actual opposition,
though, was led by Mr J. F. Alcock, captain of the
Forest Football Club, which was formed in 1859,
and was practically the first football combination
in London on anything like a proper basis.
Mr E. C. Morley, of the Barnes club, the Hon.
Secretary of the Association, however, opened the
attack with the objection that though he was of
opinion that hacking was more dreadful in name
and on paper than in reality, if it were introduced
no one who had arrived at years of discretion
would play the game, and that, in consequence, it
would be entirely relinquished to schoolboys.

Mr Campbell's counterblast in favour of hacking
was not lacking in force, and it may be interesting
to reproduce his arguments verbatim.

'Hacking,' he said, 'was the true football game,
and if you looked into the Winchester records
you would find that in former years men were so
wounded, that two of them were actually carried
off the field, and they allowed two others to occupy
their places and finish the game.' Lately, however,
the game had become more civilised than that state
of things, which certainly was to a certain extent

brutal. As to not liking hacking as at present carried on, he thought they had no business to draw up such a rule at Cambridge, and that it savoured far more of the feelings of those who liked their pipes and grog or schnaps more than the manly game of football. He was of the opinion that the reason why they objected to hacking was because too many of the members of the clubs began late in life, and were too old for that spirit of the game, which is so fully entered into at the public schools and by public schoolmen in later life. If you did away with hacking, he foretold that all the courage and pluck of the game would be done away with; and he finally created great amusement by suggesting that he would bring over a lot of Frenchmen, who would beat the exponents of the proposed code with a week's practice.

Mr Campbell's realistic feature of the delights of hacking, however, did not seem to have any appreciable effect and, indeed, the rule providing a penalty for its practice was carried by thirteen to four.

Intimation had meanwhile been given by those representing the non-contents that, in the event of the rejection of the principle of hacking the Blackheath party would be compelled to secede, and the formal notification of the withdrawal of the Blackheath club was duly made at the following meeting, held at the Freemasons Tavern on 8 December 1863. The new code adopted on that occasion, while admitting for a try at goal, had disallowed running with the ball and passing, as well as tripping and hacking. The first of these was, of course, the *raison d'être* of the Rugby game, and the abolition of running would have meant such a radical alteration in the constitution of football that it can hardly be a surprise to find those who had been educated in the mysteries of that particular kind of game opposed to a sweeping reform, which would have reduced them to the necessity of unlearning the lessons of their boyhood, and schooling themselves in a, to a great extent, different game. The withdrawal of the Blackheath club from the Football Association, 8 December 1863, destroyed the last remaining hope of an assimilation of existing differences. Since that time football players have been divided into two great camps, the one favouring the Association, the other the Rugby game, wide as the poles asunder, though at the same time perfectly friendly rivals.

The code of 8 December 1863, the first issued by the Football Association, will be interesting as indicative of the comparatively slight changes that have been made in the Association game since it first became popular thirty years ago.

1. The maximum length of the ground shall be 200 yards; the maximum breadth shall be 100 yards; the length and breadth shall be marked off with flags; and the goal shall be defined by two upright posts, 8 yards apart, without any tape or bar across them.

2. A toss for goals shall take place, and the game shall be commenced by a place kick from the centre of the ground by the side losing the toss. The other side shall not approach within ten yards of the ball until it is kicked off.

3. After a goal is won, the losing side shall be entitled to kick off, and the two sides shall change goals after each goal is won.

4. A goal shall be won when the ball passes between the goalposts or over the space between the goalposts (at whatever height), not being thrown, knocked on, or carried.

5. When the ball is in touch, the first player who touches it shall throw it from the point on the boundary line where it left the ground in a direction at right angles with the boundary line, and the ball shall not be in play until it has touched the ground.

6. When a player has kicked the ball, any one of the same side who is nearer to the opponent's goal line is out of play, and may not touch the ball himself, nor in any way whatsoever prevent any other player from doing so until he is in play; but no player is out of play when the ball is kicked off from behind the goal line.

7. In case the ball goes behind the goal line, if a player on the side to whom the goal belongs first touches the ball, one of his side shall be entitled to a free-kick from the goal line at the point opposite the place where the ball shall be touched. If a player of the opposite side first touches the ball, one of his side shall be entitled to a free-kick at the goal, only from a point fifteen yards outside the goal line, opposite the place where the ball is touched, the opposing side standing within the goal line until he has had his kick.

8. If a player makes a fair catch, he shall be entitled to a free-kick, providing he claims it by making a mark with his heel at once;

and in order to take such kick he may go as far back as he pleases, and no player on the opposite side shall advance beyond his mark until he has kicked.

9. No player shall run with the ball.
10. Neither tripping nor hacking shall be allowed, and no player shall use his hands to hold or push his adversary.
11. A player shall not be allowed to throw the ball or pass it to another with his hands.
12. No player shall be allowed to take the ball from the ground with his hands under any pretence whatever while it is in play.
13. No player shall be allowed to wear projecting nails, iron plates, or gutta-percha on the soles or heels of his boots.

## Definition of Terms

A PLACE KICK is a kick at the ball while it is on the ground, in any position that the kicker may choose to place it.

A FREE-KICK is the privilege of kicking the ball, without obstruction, in such manner as the kicker may think fit.

A FAIR CATCH is when the ball is caught, after it has touched the person of an adversary, or has been kicked or knocked on by an adversary, and before it has touched the ground or one of the side catching it; but if the ball is kicked behind the goal line, a fair catch cannot be made.

HACKING is kicking an adversary.

TRIPPING is throwing an adversary by the use of the legs.

HOLDING includes the obstruction of a player by the hand or any part of the arm below the elbow.

TOUCH is that part of the field, on either side of the ground, which is beyond the line of flags.

# 2

# The Growth of the Association Game

As has been pointed out in the previous chapter, the formation of the Association as an independent body, with a code of its own, practically dates from 8 December 1863. The withdrawal of the Blackheath club meant the withdrawal of all the clubs favouring Rugby rules, and their secession left the management of the Association in the hands of those who had advocated the adoption of the dribbling game. Mr Campbell had consented to retain the post of Treasurer until the next annual meeting; and his retirement destroyed the last link of union between the followers of the two great schools of football. As a consequence, it was not long before the few vestiges of the Rugby game, which had been incorporated in the first code, framed by the executive of the Association, were removed. At the very next general meeting, held in February 1866, the try at goal was displaced. The touchdown, though, was still retained for a time, and in the event of no goals being scored, or an equal number obtained by each side, a match could be decided by a majority of touch-downs. At the same time, with a view apparently to secure the co-operation of Westminster and Charterhouse, the strict offside rule that had been in force was modified to ensure uniformity in this essential principle of the game. The adoption of the rule that had prevailed at these two schools, which kept a player onside as long as there were three of the opposite side between him and the enemy's goal, removed, in fact, the one remaining bar to the establishment of one universal code for Association players, in the south at least. In the north, Sheffield maintained a code of its own, and some years elapsed before the Sheffield Association gave up its own rules, and thereby gave the parent Association undivided and undisputed control as the legislators of the game.

Meanwhile, in the early part of 1866, a suggestion had been received from the Hon. Secretary of the Sheffield club that a match should be played between London and Sheffield. The challenge, it is hardly necessary to add, was duly accepted, and the match, the first of any importance under the auspices of the Football Association, took place in Battersea Park in the spring of 1866. The Wanderers – practically a continuation of the Forest Football Club, which changed its name in 1863 after four years of unbroken success – Barnes, Crystal Palace, and NNs were then the backbone of the Association game in the neighbourhood of London. These four clubs between them furnished the eleven which represented London. As the names may be of interest, the Wanderers supplied four – C. W. Alcock, R. D. Elphinstone, Quintin Hogg, and J. A. Boyson; Barnes three – J. K. Barnes, R. G. Graham, and R. W. Willis; the NNs the same number in A. J. Baker, A. Pember, and C. M. Tebbut; while the eleventh place, and that one the most important, the responsible position of goalkeeper, was filled by a member of the Crystal Palace club, Alec Morten, who for some years, veteran though he was, had no superior between the posts.

Mr E. C. Morley, the first Hon. Secretary, in the interim had been replaced by another member of the Barnes club, in Mr R. W. Willis, who in turn gave way to still a third representative of Barnes in the person of Mr R. G. Graham.

The success that had attended the meeting between London and Sheffield had contributed in no small measure to increase the popularity of the Association game in London, and the effects were visible in a considerable addition to the number of clubs that declared allegiance to the Association.

The winter of 1867, too, saw another step in the development of the game – the institution of County matches. Middlesex at the time possessed a large proportion of the principal players within the Metropolitan area, and Middlesex was considered strong enough of itself to meet a combination of Surrey and Kent. It was a clever handicap, too, for the match, which took place on 2 November 1867 in Battersea Park instead of Beaufort House, the use of which had been promised for the purpose, and, for some unaccountable reason or other, withdrawn at the last moment, ended, after a most stubbornly contested game, in a draw without goals to either side. A few months later, Surrey and Kent met at the West London Running Grounds, Brompton, a match that was the forerunner of the Inter-County contests that have been continued with increasing success down to the present date.

Even at this time, the sphere of the Association was very limited. On 1 January 1868, only twenty-eight clubs owned its jurisdiction. These were the Amateur Athletic, Barnes, Bramham College (Yorkshire), Charterhouse School, Civil Service, C.C.C. (Clapham), Cowley School (Oxford), Crystal Palace, Donington Grammar School

(Lincolnshire), Forest School (Walthamstow), Holt (Wilts), Hull College, Hitchin, Kensington School, Leamington College, London Scottish Rifles, London Athletic, Milford College (South Wales), NNs (Kilburn), Royal Engineers (Chatham), Reigate, Sheffield, Totteridge Park (Herts), Upton Park, Wanderers, Westminster School, West Brompton College, and Worlabye House (Roehampton).

The wants, too, of the Association were evidently of the smallest, as at the general meeting held on 26 February 1868 it was deemed expedient to institute an annual subscription of five shillings, and a record on the minutes of that same meeting is not without significance, containing as it does the announcement that there were no funds in hand, and no balance sheet was read.

Still, by this time the Association had become firmly established, and by the spring of 1870 it was already commencing to develop its resources. The month of February in that year had seen the retirement of Mr R. G. Graham from the position of Hon. Secretary, and the election in his stead of Mr C. W. Alcock, who was subsequently replaced by Mr F. J. Wall, the present secretary. It was just about this period, too, that the Sheffield Association decided to assimilate its rules to those of the parent society – the only step required to realise the long-expected hope of one code of rules acknowledged by Association players throughout the kingdom. In the first half of the seventies, indeed, the Association was making history in bounds.

Another important event in the annals of the Association was foreshadowed during the summer of 1871. At a meeting of the committee, held on 20 July in that year, it was resolved 'that it is desirable that a Challenge Cup should be established in connection with the Association, for which all clubs should be invited to compete'. The idea was received with general favour. At a subsequent meeting, held on 16 October 1871, attended by, in addition to the committee, representatives of the Royal Engineers, Barnet, Wanderers, Harrow Chequers, Clapham Rovers, Hampstead Heathens, Civil Service, Crystal Palace, Upton Park, Windsor House Park, and Lausanne clubs, the resolution was carried 'that a Challenge Cup be established, open to all clubs belonging to the Football Association'. Owing to the fact that most of the fixture cards had been completed for the season, the northern clubs were conspicuous by their absence. Sixteen clubs in all had entered, and of these only two – Queen's Park Club, Glasgow, and Donington Grammar School – came from north of Hertfordshire. Hitchin, the Royal Engineers, Reigate Priory, Maidenhead and Great Marlow were all outside the Metropolitan radius; but the other eight – the Wanderers, Harrow Chequers, Barnes, Civil Service, Crystal Palace, Upton Park, the Clapham Rovers, and Hampstead Heathens – were all within easy reach of the city, and all came fairly under the category of London clubs.

The insertion in the first rule of a clause, giving the committee the power to exempt provincial clubs from the early tie drawings, enabled the Queen's Park club to come up fresh to London as one of the four competitors in the fourth round. Their opponents were the Wanderers, and the match, the first of a really international character under the Association rules, was played at Kennington Oval and ended in a draw. Unfortunately, they were unable to stay in London to replay the game, and the Wanderers, who thus qualified for the final, were successful in winning the trophy for the first time, after a stiff contest with the Royal Engineers, by one goal to none, though they had all the best of the play.

I specially stated that the meeting between the Wanderers and Queen's Park was the first that could be called a bona fide international match for a particular reason. For some time past there had been contests bearing the title of England *v.* Scotland in London, but, as a matter of fact, the eleven that represented Scotland were, in a great measure, composed of players merely of Scotch extraction, and in some cases, perhaps, of even less substantial qualifications. The successful show made by the Queen's Park club against the Wanderers in the competition for the Football Association Cup was, beyond a doubt, mainly responsible for 'the institution of an international match between England and Scotland on a strict basis'. The very suggestion of such a contest under Association rules was quite enough to rouse the ire of the Rugby players north of the Tweed. At the time, indeed, the Rugby game was paramount in Scotland. All the principal clubs played according to Rugby rules, and, in fact, the Queen's Park eleven was the only combination, I think I am right in saying, in the country that had adopted the Association game. The captains of the Scotch Rugby clubs were determined, too, not to have their rights usurped without at least a protest. A letter, signed by representatives of the leading clubs in Glasgow and Edinburgh, appeared in the *Scotsman* newspaper, pointing out the absurdity of Scotland taking part in an international match under rules that were not in favour with the bulk of Scottish football players. There was, of course, a good deal of sense in the objection, but, as was only to be expected, it did not have any effect in checking the advance of the Association game. On the contrary, the opposition only gave a new zest to the efforts of the promoters of the movement, and the preliminaries were not only ratified, but the match duly decided at Glasgow on 30 November 1872.

The game, which was played on the ground of the West of Scotland Cricket Club in Glasgow, proved to be singularly well contested, and, in fact, the two elevens were so very evenly weighted that at the end of an hour and a half neither had been able to secure a goal. The Football Association could hardly have had a better advertisement, and the enterprise of those who had been mainly responsible for the ratification of the match was fully rewarded by the great impetus it gave to the diffusion of Association rules throughout the west of Scotland. A return match was brought off at the end of the same season at Kennington Oval, when England won by four goals to one. Since that time, only one fixture has been made for each winter, with a great advantage to Scotland, who, until the last twenty years, had an almost uninterrupted sequence of victories.

The satisfactory completion of this first international match marked a new era in Association football, and the effects were, as was only to be expected, far-reaching. In Scotland, the Rugby game soon found itself faced by a formidable rival. New clubs were formed in all parts, with every sign of vitality. On every available open space youngsters found amusement in urging the flying ball, so that there was a constant accession of likely players to disseminate the game all over the country. The development of the Association game in Scotland was indeed extraordinary, and in the course of a few years the enthusiasm of the Queen's Park club had worked such a wonderful effect, that the Rugby element, which had for so long enjoyed a monopoly of Scotch football, was already in a minority.

By this time, the future of the Association game was well assured. The fusion of the Sheffield Association rules with those of the parent body removed the last remaining obstacle in the way of a universal code for players of that way of thinking. Since then, though the constitution of the Association has undergone several, and most of them important, changes, the game itself remains very much the game it was, with only some very slight modifications, with the object of repressing the excess of zeal that has been, perhaps, the rational outcome of the growth of the game, and of the keen competition that has followed the rapid development of football during the last few years. The changes in the constitution of the Association, and the chief events that have marked the devolution of Association football, will form material for a special chapter.

# 3

# The Progress of the Association

The withdrawal of the party that affected the Rugby game, following so closely as it did on the well-meant attempt of those who were chiefly responsible for the foundation of the Football Association to devise a code that should be acceptable to both parties, naturally slowed the advance of the Association. For some time the policy of those who guided its destinies in its infancy was mainly of a passive kind. The first object was to conciliate the different schools that had shown themselves averse to the adoption of Rugby rules. It was not an easy task to incorporate the many different varieties of the dribbling game then in vogue into one comprehensive scheme. The work was necessarily slow, and for several years the history of the Association was singularly uneventful. By degrees, though, the process of absorption took effect, and as the influence of the Association extended, there was a corresponding willingness among those who had before adhered to their own particular variation of the game to recognise the importance, if not the necessity, of a uniform set of rules.

Prominent among those who helped consolidate the Association in its early days, and to establish it on a permanent basis, may be mentioned three keen football players – Messrs Arthur Pember, the captain of the NNs; E. C. Morley, the ruling spirit of the Barnes club; and J. Forster Alcock, captain of the Forest club, Leytonstone. It was in a great measure, indeed, to the indefatigable efforts of these three gentlemen at the outset of its career that the Association was able to surmount the numerous difficulties that interfered for a time with its advancement. The requirements of more important work soon compelled Mr Morley to give up the position of Hon. Secretary, to which he had been elected at the inaugural meeting, in favour of Mr R. W. Willis, as previously stated. The former, though, continued to do good work as one of the committee, and, on the retirement of Mr Pember, he was unanimously elected to fill the highest office, that of President. At that time the committee only consisted of four members, and in the early part of 1867, the affairs of the Association were managed by a directorate of six – the President, the Hon. Secretary and Treasurer, a dual office, and the committee, consisting of Messrs C. W. Alcock, of the Wanderers; W. J. Cutbill, of the Crystal Palace; W. Chesterman, of Sheffield; and R. W. Willis, of Barnes, who had just before given up the post of Hon. Secretary.

The earliest revision of the rules saw the abolition of the free-kick, and though a provision was at first inserted allowing a player to *stop* the ball with his hands, it was soon afterwards removed, as was, indeed, everything that could by any chance be considered to savour of the Rugby game. An attempt by the Sheffield club to introduce rouges, after the fashion of the Eton field game, met with no favour; and a modification, also proposed by Sheffield, of the strict offside rule so as to make anyone onside provided the goalkeeper alone was between them and the opposite goal was equally unsuccessful. Though the proposition that practically did away with onside altogether was not in sympathy with the feelings of the majority of the clubs, which at that time constituted the Football Association, it nonetheless for a long time retained its popularity with those who were responsible for the management of the Sheffield Association. For nearly ten winters, indeed, it formed perhaps the only important point of divergence between the rules of the parent society and the oldest, as well as the most loyal, of its affiliated Associations. The matches between London and Sheffield were originally played twice during the season, in London and Sheffield, according to the respective rules in force in each district. Subsequently, though, the fixtures became so popular that it was deemed advisable to add still a third contest of a mixed character, in one half of which London rules – i.e. those of the Football Association – governed the play, and the other conducted in accordance with the code of the Sheffield Association. Such an anomalous and unsatisfactory arrangement one would have thought could only have been of brief duration. Still, the Sheffield players were not easily persuaded to yield the few points in which their game differed from that of the central and administrative body of Association football. It was not, in fact, till the year 1876 that the rules of the Sheffield Association were brought into complete agreement with those of the original foundation, and the last obstacle in the way of a universal code for the regulation of Association players was removed.

It must not be assumed, though, that the committee of the Football Association were directly or indirectly responsible, as might perhaps be inferred from my remarks, for the arrangement or control of these early matches between London and Sheffield. They had systematically declined to recognise any modification of the rules. An offer of the Sheffield Association for a home and home match was, indeed, refused solely for this reason; and a challenge from the Cambridge University Association Football Club to play a match under the rules of that Association, was also declined. On similar ground, overtures had also been made in 1871, on behalf of the South Derbyshire Association, for a conference of the two bodies with a view to amalgamation, but this proposition met with the same lack of encouragement. Until the fusion of the Sheffield Association with the parent society, the selection and management of the London team was wholly and solely in private hands, and the fixtures had in no way the official impress of the Football Association.

Meanwhile, the establishment of a Challenge Cup, open to all clubs belonging to the Association, had, as already stated, given a great stimulus to the game. Instituted in 1871, through the initiative mainly of a few of the more influential of the Metropolitan clubs, it was not long before the Cup took a much wider scope. In the first code of rules the holders were only required to take part in the final match, but this provision was only in force for one year, and, subsequently, the club winning the Cup had to fight its way through the competition the same as the other entrants, until quite recently, when a qualifying competition was instituted to weed out the smaller clubs.

Though the introduction of Association football into Lancashire about the same period as the establishment of the Cup, the first of an innumerable succession of trophies of a similar kind was a mere coincidence and in no way connected. It is curious, considering the conspicuous part Lancashire clubs have played in the competition of late years, that their origin should have been coeval.

The paternity of the Association game in Lancashire may be claimed by Mr J. C. Kay, an old Harrovian, who subsequently made himself a reputation in another branch of sport, as a lawn tennis player of no small ability, as well as manager of perhaps the best organised lawn tennis meeting in the kingdom – that which takes place annually on the ground of the Liverpool Cricket Club. Educated at Harrow, it was only natural that the primitive game in use in Lancashire should have been based very much on the eccentric admixture of different codes to which young Harrow had been used for generation after generation. The introduction of the Association game into Lancashire was, in fact, in a very great measure the work of an old Harrovian, as, some twenty years before, the initiation of the movement that practically led to the revival of football on a proper basis was to a considerable extent the work of a few keen athletes who had graduated at his school.

To East Lancashire, in particular, belongs the credit of fostering the game in its infancy, as well as of assisting in the development that has resulted in making Lancashire one of the most powerful influences in Association football. Bolton, I believe, was the first place that took at all kindly to the new sport, and, under Mr Kay's watchful eye, the Harrow game, or perhaps as near a reproduction as could be devised to suit local requirements, for a time supplied all the wants of the lads who were undergoing their novitiate in football. Practice took place in the evenings, and, in fact, the game was of a very primitive kind, followed after the hard work of the day had been completed. It was not long, though, before an attempt was made to evolve something like a system out of the rough efforts of these pioneers of Lancashire football. The first result of this organisation, I have reason to believe, was the Bolton Wanderers club, which has outlived the many changes through which football has gone during the last quarter of a century, and still remains a power in the land; in fact, one of the most influential combinations of the same kind in the north of England.

But to return to the Cup, which has had such a material effect on the development of the Association. There has been, and still is, a large section, even of the best friends and supporters of football, who take exception to Cup competitions. Their objection of course is, not to the Cup itself, but to its surroundings, or rather to its accompaniments, or to what they are used to call its incidental evils. The good folk who hold these opinions have, it must be admitted, a certain amount of reason to support their arguments. But their policy is at the best one of ultramarine, the bluest of the blue, the policy of conservatism of the most pronounced type.

Their contention is, in the main, that Cup competitions give rise to an excessive rivalry. According to their notions, the stimulus they give is not conducive to the real interests of the game. On the contrary, the desire to secure possession of, or even to gain a prominent place in the struggle for, the Cup, they impute, introduces an unhealthy feeling, which not only tempts the clubs to make the well-being of the game subservient to their own particular interests, but tends to lower the general standard of morality among those who compete. There could hardly be a more sweeping indictment, and were there any real justification, public opinion, one would have thought, would have asserted itself in unmistakable terms in disapproval. The evils that are supposed to follow in the train of Cup competitions, according to those who view them with disfavour, had they been actual, would indeed have long since produced the abolition instead of the increase of Cups all over the kingdom. As a matter of fact, though, the dangers of which these good people prate are more visionary than real; at least, they have not as yet assumed a tangible shape. The opponents of this class of football call to mind Hamlet's familiar expression, 'The lady doth protest too much, methinks.'

That Cups give rise to more than ordinary interest is a practical truth of which those who assisted in the institution of the original trophy have had abundant and increasing evidence year after year. It is only the excessive multiplication of Cups that seems to have produced any general feeling of dissatisfaction.

The fear of inordinate betting, which it was predicted would inevitably follow the establishment of such competitions, has, as far as a lengthy and intimate knowledge of the working of one of the most important of them gives any weight, not by any means been realised. Nor has there been shown to have been any reason for the assumption that participation in a Cup competition would tend *ipso facto* to deaden the sensibilities or susceptibilities of either the managers of clubs or the players.

So far at least as the experience of over thirty years goes, the trial of the Football Association Cup has been a complete refutation of the arguments of those who were opposed to its inception from the reasons referred to. The disadvantages have been few; the advantages, on the other hand, many and undeniable. No one, of course, will deny that; were the supervision lax, the outcome of the keen rivalry engendered would be abuses of the kind indicated by those who cannot see any good in developing the game by such means.

Whatever may be urged to their disadvantage, the fact remains beyond dispute that where Cup competitions have been introduced, football has not only increased in popularity, but new clubs have sprung up and, as a natural consequence, players have multiplied. The extraordinary development of the Association game during the last fifteen years is beyond all doubt attributable in a very great measure to the influence of *the* Cup. It is something more than a coincidence, too, that the Rugby game is nowhere more popular than in the Midlands, one of the few districts where Rugby rules are predominant in which a Cup competition has been carried on with any energy.

Whether after a time Cups do not outlive the good they originally did, is a point outside the scope of the general argument that they have a material affect in encouraging the game and stimulating the players when encouragement and stimulant are needed. If you seek the measure of the good the Football Association Cup has done to disseminate as well as to consolidate the game, you have only to look around. Nor, as far as one can see, is there the smallest evidence to show that either those who play or the public that supports football are suffering from a surfeit in this particular direction. On the contrary, where such competitions have been conducted on proper lines there has been no diminution of interest, and indeed the older trophies, though insignificant by comparison with those of recent date, both in value and appearance, still hold their own with the best of those of later growth. The development of the game in Hampshire, and still more recently in Kent, would not have been so rapid, or have attained such proportions so quickly, had it not been for the spirit of rivalry engendered by the judicious introduction of a spirit of competition, which not only gave a stimulus to the clubs already formed in populous towns like Chatham and Woolwich, but also emboldened the more ardent spirits in the outlying districts to form aggregations of players not unfrequently scattered over a wide area who would probably have had no chance of consolidation, unless by very slow process, but for the extraneous influences that necessitated the adoption of a system of combination, the outcome of the same spirit of rivalry that has made Inter-County or international matches the keenest of all contests.

I have gone into the subject of Cup competitions and their effects on the game at some length, because it must be conceded that for good or evil they have played an important part in the history of Association football. Nor will anyone, I fancy, be bold enough to dispute that the institution of the parent Cup in 1863 was practically the initiation of a new policy that had very important bearings on the future of the game.

A record of Association football without some attempt to revive the memories of those who

worked so hard to assure the early success of the
Football Association Cup, and thereby to lay
the foundation of the prosperity of the Association,
would be utterly incomplete. The events that led
to the inception of the trophy have been already
referred to, the names of the clubs to whom its
institution was practically due have been given. At
that time the Wanderers monopolised the cream of
the public school and University players for some
years. To have graduated at one of the leading
schools or at one of the two great Universities
was an essential qualification for membership,
though the rules were subsequently relaxed so
as to admit the introduction of a limited number
of outsiders.

In the earlier days of the Cup, the Wanderers
were really the most influential body in Association
football, and their record was one of exceptional
brilliance. In the first seven years after the Cup
was constituted, it was held by the Wanderers five
times; and though they won it outright by three
successive victories in 1876, 1877, and 1878, they
returned it to the Association, which thereupon
framed a rule enacting that it shall never become
the permanent property of any team.

The gradual enrolment of clubs composed
exclusively of old public school boys struck at the
very roots of the Wanderers' constitution; and,
though it still continues in name, it ceased to be a
power, and, indeed, was practically disbanded some
years ago. Since its disappearance, though the Old
Etonians, Clapham Rovers, and Carthusians have
each had the distinction of holding it, latterly the
possession of the Cup has been in the hands of
northern teams mainly composed of professional
players. The Blackburn Rovers, emulating the

achievement of the Wanderers, won it three times in succession (in 1884, 1885, and 1886); and that club secured it subsequently in 1890 and 1891, making five times in all, equalling in this, too, the record of the Wanderers. Since the latter year the Cup has, with one notable exception, been held by Midland or Northern clubs. Aston Villa's victory, in 1905, was their fourth up to date. Tottenham Hotspurs, who won in 1901 after a drawn game, is the only Southern team that has won it since 1882, although Southampton were the runners-up in 1900 and 1902, and in the latter year only went down after a drawn game.

Unfortunately, Aston Villa's recollections of the early Cup fights must always be dimmed by one unpleasant memory. This was the theft of the original Cup from a shop window in Birmingham while it was in their possession as holders in 1905. As all attempts to recover it or to trace those who stole it were futile, the only alternative for the Football Association was to provide a replica, which is the trophy for which clubs compete and have competed for the last ten years. Though they did not get home in the first year of the new Cup, Aston Villa secured it in 1897, and again in 1905. Of the winners in the middle ages of the Cup, though comparisons are proverbially odious, the Preston North End team of 1889 stand out perhaps most conspicuously by reason of their all-round football. Like Aston Villa eight winters later, they won the League Championship when it was just instituted without losing a match in 1889, and also the Football Association Cup without having a goal scored against them. Though latterly they have not been able to reproduce the brilliant form they showed under the watchful eye of their great supporter, Mr Sudell, the memories of their consistently fine football two decades or so ago are still fresh. What a hold the Cup final has on the football public as a spectacle cannot be better illustrated than by a mere mention of the fact that no less than 110,802 persons visited the Crystal Palace in 1901 to see Tottenham Hotspurs, the ultimate winners, and Sheffield United play a drawn game.

Incidental reference to Preston North End's double first in 1889 recalls the formation of the Football League, the creation of a lifelong worker in Association football, Mr W. McGregor, early that season. What an important part the League system has played in the economy of modern football can hardly be fully discussed in what is primarily a practical treatise on the game. It certainly came originally to supply a general and obvious want in the shape of a competition of continuous interest, and not like the FA Cup, with a glorious uncertainty to all the clubs concerned. No history of Association football would be complete if full justice were not done to the great influence of the League, and the hundreds of kindred combinations founded on the same lines and carried on with such remarkable success all over the country.

Another movement that has done much to consolidate the Association game was the institution of the Amateur Cup competition. For reasons best known to themselves, a section of the more influential of the southern amateur teams, notably the Old Boys' clubs, have latterly held aloof from the competition. One would have thought, in the interests of the game, they would have been the most keen to encourage. Still, there are signs that the Amateur Cup may yet thoroughly fulfil its mission, and the entries during the last two or three years have shown a great improvement in quality as well as quantity. The policy of the FA in instituting international matches for amateurs with the other European nations will, too, undoubtedly lead to the development and consolidation of amateur football.

# 4

# The Football of Today

Though the requirements necessary to attain excellence on the football field are in the main precisely the same today as they were twenty years ago, the whole character of the game is as different as the old style of the Rugby game, with its heavy forwards and its wearisome scrummages, is to the new order, with its rapid changes, its lighter and faster forwards, its looser scrummages, and the recent development of passing among the backs, which has added so much to the popularity of Rugby rules during the last few years. Pluck, energy, weight and quickness of decision are quite as valuable attributes for the football player as they ever were. The evolution of football, though, has necessitated not only a revision of the general system of play, but an entire rearrangement of the whole principle of the game – a complete alteration in the distribution of the players, as well as in the composition of the eleven. In the old times there were infinitely more opportunities for the exhibition of individual skill, and in some respects perhaps an Association match of thirty years ago was more interesting to watch for that particular reason. A skilful dribbler was then by no means a rarity, on the contrary, to dribble well was one of the chief ends of a forward's football education. It was necessary, as well, to be a good shot at goal, and these two qualities were essential to the attainment of any great degree of excellence as a forward in the sixties, and, in fact, until well into the seventies.

The arrangement of an eleven in those times was directed rather to strengthen the attack than to procure a stout defence. The tendency was certainly to favour the forwards rather than to encourage the backs. The formation of a team as a rule, indeed, was to provide for seven forwards, and only four players to constitute the three lines of defence. The last line was, of course, the goalkeeper and in front of him was only one full-back, who had again before him but two half-backs, to check the rushes of the opposite forwards. Under the old style of play, this formation was not so dangerous as it might appear to one of the modern school of football. Dribbling had been chiefly encouraged at the schools, from which the game sprang, and purely individual play remained for a long time one of the chief features of an Association match. There was some little attempt at passing, of course, but a good dribbler stuck to the ball as long as he could, especially if he saw a reasonably good chance of outrunning the three backs, who formed the only obstacles he had to overcome. Long runs were frequent, and as a consequence individual skill was in a great measure the source of a football reputation.

To be a good dribbler was the Alpha and Omega of the forward's creed in the early days of Association football. At the same time, it must not be understood that he was unprovided with support in case of any obstruction in the course of a run. There was the provision, of course, of backing up, i.e. of a player who followed up the ball ready either to receive the ball if it were passed to him, or to hustle or ward off any interference by the opposite forwards or backs. Still, at the best, backing up existed more in theory than practice. The dribbler, indeed, lingered long on the football field, even some time after he had ceased to be a potential factor in the game. Even as late as the commencement of the eighties – though some years before the forwards had been reduced to admit an addition to the defence in the shape of a second full-back – the advantages of dribbling were still represented in forcible terms by one of the earliest instructors in the art of football. This is a part of the advice he gave to forwards in the winter of 1878:

A really first-class player – I am now addressing myself solely to those who play up – will never lose sight of the ball, at the same time keeping his attention employed in spying out any gaps in the enemy's ranks, or any weak points in the defence, which may give him a favourable chance of arriving at the coveted goal. To see some players guide and steer a ball through a circle of opposing legs, turning and twisting as occasion requires, is a sight not to be forgotten; and this faculty or aptitude for guiding the ball often places a slow runner on an equal footing with one much speedier of foot. Speed is not an indispensable ingredient in the formation of a 'good dribbler', though undoubtedly fleetness of foot goes far to promote success. Skill in dribbling, though, necessitates something more than a go-ahead, fearless, headlong onslaught on the enemy's citadel; it requires an eye quick at discovering a weak point, and nous to calculate and decide the chances of a successful passage.

The footballer of today will bear with us, it is to be hoped, in the attempt to portray, for the benefit of posterity, a type of the old school – 'a poor player', to use Macbeth's phrases, 'that struts and frets his hour upon the stage, and then is heard no more.' The quotation just given from the *Football Annual* will show that, even then, when the seventies were on the wane, the dribbler's occupation was rapidly going, and that he was steadily undergoing a process of absorption in the general reconstruction of the football field.

An important alteration in the rules, enacting that the ball ought to be thrown out from touch in any direction instead of, as hitherto, thrown out straight, carried in 1877, marked a new era in the history of Association football. Mention is made incidentally of this change, because, though it did not become law without strenuous opposition all along the line, it tended to make the game so much faster, that it really, in some measure, helped to expedite the material revolution that was taking place in the Association game was at least contemporaneous with the first sign of the transition through which football was passing. 'What was ten or fifteen years ago the recreation of a few,' to quote again from the *Football Annual*, 'has now become the pursuit of thousands – an athletic exercise, carried on under a strict system and, in many cases, by an enforced term of training, almost magnified into a profession.' Here was the first note of the transformation the game was slowly undergoing, and the *Annual* plaintively called attention to the old football fogies, as likely to 'recall with no small satisfaction the days when football had not grown to be so important as to make umpires necessary, and the "gate the first subject of consideration"'.

In one respect, however, the *Football Annual* was obliged to admit that the alteration in the method of playing the Association game had been, to use its own words, 'of infinite good, in that it had merged the individual in the side'. Even then 'passing', which had been first introduced in any degree of perfection in the early matches between London and Sheffield, had been slowly but surely ousting the dribbler.

Individual excellence ceased to be the aim of the forward, and in its place a captain wisely directed his attention to the inculcation of united action. Mechanical precision was cultivated, and the extent of the combination of a team came to be the measure of its success or failure. Still, it was some time before the players in the south took really kindly to the new style of game. To them football was still an amusement uninfluenced by any considerations of 'gate', and with true conservatism they stuck to the old system, I am bound to admit, long after it had outlived its reputation. Even the example of the Scotch teams that visited London had been thrown away, and the systematic adjustment of the forwards in vogue with the Queen's Park, the Vale of Leven, and others of the leading Scotch clubs, failed for some time to make any impression on the general body of footballers in the South of England.

The rearrangement of an eleven so as to suit the alteration in the general method of play, as I have said, proved to be a very slow process. The main object of the new reforms was to strengthen the defence without sacrificing the offensive powers of a team. As it was, the introduction of the passing game revolutionised the forward play to such a degree that it was quite possible to spare one of the forwards without materially weakening the attack.

The formation of an eleven in the early days of Association football was a premium on forward play, and the backs were for a long time, to all intents and purposes, ignored. To be a good dribbler, as well as a safe, short passer, was the perfection of art when the game was in its infancy. It is hardly to be wondered at that this should have been the highest possible development of football at the time, for the bulk of the players were merely carrying out a system that had been inculcated at the public schools. Under the original constitution, indeed, there was little to encourage the cultivation of defensive play. At first an eleven was constituted of eight forwards, one back, one half-back, and a goalkeeper; and even at a later date, where there was practically no offside, the player who had charge of the posts had about as thankless a position as it would be possible to conceive.

This method of distributing the players, however, did not last very long. It soon became evident that the policy was not the most conducive to the best interests of the game. A player possessed of great pace, as well as capable of working the ball with any degree of dexterity, when he once got away, had practically little or no obstruction to overcome, and if, in addition to the qualities named, he was a fairly sure shot when in front of goal, in a majority of cases a run could be counted on to result in a certain score. Time, however, has changed all that.

The first move in this direction was to withdraw the third centre to furnish a second full-back – an absolute necessity – to meet the additional strain on the defence caused by the development of the passing system. The adoption of the extra full-back for a time satisfied the requirements of the older school of football players at least. Some time, indeed, elapsed before there was any movement in the direction of a further limitation of the forwards. So late as 1874 the original arrangement of an eleven, consisting of seven forwards, two half-backs, a full-back, and a goalkeeper, was still in force, and the writer of an article on the Association game, published not very long since, pointed out that this was the principle on which the two elevens were constituted in the Inter-University match of that year. The appearance of the second full-back was an afterthought, at least in England, and it was not until the following winter that he came to be regarded as a recognised appendage to an eleven.

Meanwhile, the principal Scotch clubs had already begun to see the importance of still greater reform, to meet the change that had gradually been altering the whole tone of the game. They had long before tried, and successfully, the practice of systematic passing, and the disappearance of the dribbler was the logical outcome of the change. Under the new dispensation, it was necessary that the eleven should work on a definite system, and with a mechanical precision that had hitherto been unknown. Each player had his allotted station; he was, in fact, an integral part of a machine that could not work smoothly unless every section was fitted to a nicety and the gear properly adjusted.

So far the reformers were satisfied with a fairly equal distribution of the attack and the defence, and for some time the general practice was to constitute an eleven of six forwards and five backs. As the principle of passing, however, came to be more fully understood, and the attack grew more open, it became more and more evident that the first line of defence was even yet hardly sufficient to cope with the increased rapidity of the game. As the dribbler pure and simple became extinct, and the individual became absorbed in the general mechanism of the side, the selfish player not only grew at first to be an object of distrust, but practically in course of time ceased to have a place in the internal economy of football. The transition, however, from the era of the individual player to the adoption of a constructive combination, gave rise to many interesting experiments of different kinds.

The Queen's Park team were the first to demonstrate the possibilities of combination. In the main they favoured a system of short passing, and it was in a great measure the readiness with which the Scotch players adapted themselves to the new idea that enabled Scotland to show to so much greater advantage in its international matches with England for many years. At the same time, the credit of introducing passing must not be ascribed altogether to the Scotchmen. The rules affected by the Sheffield Association gave rise to a loose and disjointed game, which directly encouraged the adoption of a certain kind of passing, and, in fact, the main feature of the general play of Sheffield teams was the transmission of the ball from one player to another, according to their stations, arranged on a definite plan.

The example of the Sheffield players was not lost on their neighbours, and a combination of some kind or other was cultivated among the other northern districts. East Lancashire had meanwhile taken up the Association game with enthusiasm. Just about the time when passing began to be considered essential to the success of a team, Blackburn furnished two clubs, both of which played an important part in the competition for the Football Association Cup. As far as I can remember, the first English team to give any exhibition of a systematic passing game in London was the Blackburn Olympic, when they won the Cup in the spring of 1883 at the Oval. The tactics of the Olympic were altogether different to those that had found favour with the Scotchmen, and though they demonstrated a new possibility, it was not of a kind to secure the approval of southern players. Their game was an alternation of long passing and vigorous rushes, which, effective enough as it proved as a novelty, and under the favourable circumstances of that particular match, did not impress the majority of southern players as likely to be the best possible style of play under every conceivable condition of ground and weather.

I have been at some pains to show the chief incidents that marked the evolution of the Association game. The leaders in the movement that gave rise to the scientific game of today were, as I have already stated, Queen's Park in Scotland and the Sheffield players on this side of the Tweed. The next move – and the most important of the many changes that have taken place in the formation of a team – though, was essentially the work of English rather than of Scotch footballers. For some time before its adoption, the idea of a third half-back had been urged, and with pertinacity, by some of the best judges of the game.[1] The northern clubs, who were the first to take kindly to the passing game, had been steadily strengthening their teams by the help of players from the other side of the Tweed. They had been gradually assuming a preponderance in the working of the Association as well; and, in fact, the old order of football had been changing, giving place to new. So far as the game itself went, the result was a benefit rather than a disadvantage to Association football. The Northerners had been at least foremost in the movement that led to the latest defensive formation, the removal of the second centre-forward to occupy a position as centre-half-back, a post akin to that taken in the Eton game by the flying man. It was realised that this generally was the most responsible place in the field perhaps, if only from the fact that to fill it properly requires a combination of offensive as well as defensive skill, a capacity for attack as well as a power of defence sufficient to keep the opposite forwards at bay, and to prevent them from getting within shooting distance of his own goal as much as possible.

The credit of the introduction of the principle of combination, of which the third half-back was the keystone, belongs, as I have already said, to English players. The movement in reality originated with some of the leading amateurs in the South of England. The first team to bring the theory of combination into practice, or at least to carry it out to any degree of perfection, was the Cambridge University eleven some twenty years ago. The practical outcome of the exhibition given by Cambridge in 1883 was a general acknowledgment of the merits of the new formation.

In this connection, it is worthy of remark that the Scotch players were the most backward in accepting the third half-back, who is now considered an essential to every properly constituted eleven. The improvement in the game generally, the result of the adoption of a policy of combination, was not long in taking effect on the English players, and, indeed, it is worthy to note that since the third half-back was introduced in 1884, though the Scotchmen have been able to claim the majority of victories in their international matches with England, the positions have been changed to such an extent that in point of actual play the advantage has been decidedly on the side of England.

Indeed, in the twenty-three matches that were played from 1884 to 1906 inclusive, England has a bare majority of victories, having won nine times to eight. How far the quality of Association football in general has been improved by the, as many think, grandmotherly legislation of late years must be a matter of opinion. The great competition among the richer clubs to secure a strong side regardless of all expense has been naturally a distribution of the better players over a wider area, and a consequent levelling up of the game all over the country. On the other hand, the whole trend of legislation of late years has been to whittle down any survival of the robust methods that made football a strenuous exercise, with the result certainly of no advantage to the game as a whole. The glorification of the mechanical at the expense of the physical element in individual play has had the effect of developing an *ultra* scientific game, which, in the matter of attack at all events, is most ludicrous and certainly by comparison most ineffective. A happy mean in this as well as in other things represents the best solution.

# 5

# Modern Football, and How to Play It

From what has already been written, it will be understood that in the accepted formation of an Association eleven, according to modern notions, the main idea is to equalise as much as possible the attack and the defence.

The half-backs, if they appreciate the full measure of their responsibilities, have in great measure an offensive as well as a defensive mission; and indeed the middle half in particular has it in his power to be of very great assistance in acting as a kind of extra centre-forward. He ought, in fact, to feed the wings, when occasion arises, very much as the centre does, and, if thoroughly up to his duties, ought to be quite the most useful man in the team.

It is difficult at present to anticipate any evolution that can produce a better or more perfect combination. The eleven, it will be understood, therefore, is formed of five forwards – two players on each wing, one centre, and six to constitute the defence – three half-backs forming the first line, two full-backs behind them, and last of all the goalkeeper, on whom falls the task of checking the final assault. Perhaps, though, it will give a better idea of the arrangement, and indeed of the general adjustment, of the football field if I give a sketch of its formation.

The whole secret of success in football lies, it is almost superfluous to add, in the measure of a team's combination.

A club eleven composed of entirely mediocre players will generally make a good show against, if it does not actually beat, a coalition of members of different bodies of vastly superior capacity individually. There is no royal road to football, and the first lesson that a young footballer must take to heart and learn thoroughly is unselfishness. It is essential that he should grasp as the fundamental principle of the game a complete abnegation of self in the interests of the side. He is, as I have said, a section of a machine that cannot act properly unless even the minutest part does its work to a nicety and in harmony. A selfish player, one who enters a football field with the idea of contributing purely to self-glorification, will very soon find himself out in the cold, and his place filled by one who is more capable of advancing the general well-being of his side. Combination is the only possible way to the attainment of anything like perfection of working in a football team, and the sooner the tyro recognises the importance of mastering this first lesson, the sooner will he be on the way to advancement.

# 6

# The Captaincy

The capacity of the football machine is, as will be gathered from the foregoing remarks, dependent on the measure of the motor power, which is strong or weak accordingly as it is well directed and in capable hands. The efficiency of an eleven is generally in proportion to the power and skill of its captain, and it goes without saying that the appointment to fill the post should not be lightly made, and the choice fall on a player merely on account of his personal skill. The qualities required for the proper fulfilment of a post requiring peculiar skill are not inherent; they are, in fact, a gift. The power and ability to command are not given to everyone; and as the greater applies to the less, the capacity for directing even a football eleven, whose success is mainly dependent on discipline, is in its way as much a talent as the ability of a general in matters of military strategy.

If an eleven has confidence, and places implicit reliance in its captain, it has already one of the necessary elements of prosperity. As a rule, on much the same principle that a wicketkeeper is best placed to direct the field, by the mere fact of his position, which gives him the best chance of observing the greater part of the field, it is better that the captain should be a defensive rather than an offensive player. He is placed much more advantageously than a forward to grasp the weak points of the enemy, while at the same time carefully disposing his own forces to the best possible purpose. The extent of a captain's fitness will be the amount of power he wields. A competent commander naturally ensures a better system of organisation and more ready obedience even among the less tractable members. In any case, though, a captain, whatever his merits for the position, should be an autocrat on the field. He is, or should be, responsible for the behaviour and decorum of his men, and his power, while he is in charge of the side, should be absolute. A team whose members do not support its chief, but question his actions at the smallest provocation, is altogether wanting in discipline, and lacks one of the great elements of success. To sum up the question of captaincy, the fitness for the position should be clearly established before the selection is made. When once chosen, however, his position should be recognised without demur, and his orders during the game, if a side is to work well and harmoniously, implicitly carried out

Having dealt with the most important member of a football team, it will be necessary to consider, in the first place, the best measures for filling to the best advantage the various positions the players under his command will have to occupy, and secondly, the duties each will have to carry out to make the combination effective. For the better comprehension of these two matters, it will be most convenient, as well as, I think, more useful, to the beginner at all events, to subdivide the attack and the defence, with a view to a fuller explanation of the different responsibilities.

# 7

# The Forwards

The theory of forward play is, of course, to make the attack as powerful as it can possibly be without placing any undue stress on any particular part, or giving more than his fair share of the work to any individual member. The ruling principle must be a system of co-operation between the five players to produce the most effective possible working. The wings should be carefully selected with regard to their special qualifications to play outside or inside – and it is hardly necessary to add that there are special qualifications in each case in the shape of a left-footed player for the left wing, and vice versa, of fleetness of foot for the outer place, and suchlike. It is essential that there should be a thorough understanding between the five, otherwise much of the labour is wasted. To ensure an approach to perfection, the passing must be on a definite principle, and one in which the wings and the centre are thoroughly in accord. On this 'hang', indeed, 'the law and the prophets'. Something more than mere unselfishness, I may point out, is requisite to be of real use. A forward may be the very opposite of selfish, but, at the same time, if he parts with the hall injudiciously and without carefully watching the movement of his own forwards, and weighing the possibilities of his passing in relation to them, his assistance is of a negative character, and, in fact, he has often been of greater service to the opposite side. A well-constituted forward team is indeed the thoroughness of mechanical precision. The attainment of a high standard in this direction is, however, it will be readily understood, only the outcome of careful thought and constant practice. Forwards, however, one and all, should be quick on the ball, as well as with their feet, full of resolution, and with plenty of decision. Modern football does not necessitate the exceptional amount of skill in dribbling that was essential to the attainment of any great reputation thirty years ago. The change in the general character of the game has caused the dribbler pure and simple to become extinct, but still dribbling is necessary to the education of a football player now, though not of paramount importance, as it was then. Nor is the possession of physical force a *sine qua non* as it was in the early days of the great football revival. A player, to reach a position of any prominence, must be of good constitution and, withal, have plenty of stamina to enable him to hold his own in face of the extreme pace of a game from start to finish as it is nowadays. What I am trying to point out, though, is that tactical skill has more to do, in the present-day arrangement, with the attainment of success than of old.

Football culture, in fact, now requires perhaps a higher combination of talents, and the scientific tactics of an Association eleven of today are only the natural development of thought and experience. The best elevens of late years have emphatically been those who have been managed on a system carefully thought out and the result of wise elaboration. The first application of any real method in the attack, in the south at least, was by W. N. Cobbold, the old Carthusian, during his captaincy of the Cambridge University eleven of 1885. One of the most skilful forwards of the modern school, he was the first, as far as my knowledge goes, to evolve the mechanical precision that has been continued by his successors in office, and bids fair to be perpetuated in Cambridge elevens. His opinions on combination in attack are, too, of such value that it will be of interest to reproduce a portion of them for the benefit in particular of those who have passed through the preliminary stages of Association football.

The first idea of any forward should be that he is only a connecting link in a chain that should, as a rule, be kept in line, and that the whole secret of good play lies in combination.

As regards actual combination, my firm belief is that a judicious mixture of long and short passing is the most effective. If the ball be near one's own goal, let it be at once transferred to the outside right or left, as the case may be, and let him, in conjunction with his partner, go down the wing. When the time comes for middling (unless occasion shall have arisen before for him to pass), let him send the ball hard right across, along the ground if possible, or close to it, thus giving the centre and the other wing men all a chance. The time for middling comes, as a rule, some time before the goal line is reached, for a forward should rarely, if ever, try to get round the last back, but middle just before he comes to him. How often is a really good run down the wing spoilt by a middle coming too late, when the backs have returned to defend the goal, or by a high centre, which an opposing back has no difficulty in heading away! Each forward must be always ready to receive the ball, and particularly let the centre place himself judiciously, so that an inside man can give him a pass when he is clear from the centre half-back. With regard to passing, a good forward must, of course, be able to pass with both the inside and outside of his feet, and it is the knowledge that the forward can do so, which, in a great measure, puzzles the opposing half-back or back, as he cannot be sure which way the forward is going to pass. This is especially useful for short passing, when the great object is to pass quickly and accurately, yet going at full speed.

With regard to long passing, which, as I have said, may be judiciously mixed with the short, let it be done directly one sees one of the outside men with a clear opening. Often, when a good run is being made by one of the wings, the backs on the other side gradually come across and leave the extreme part of their own side quite unguarded. This is the time for a hard pass – some forty or fifty yards, it may be. With regard to all passing, the forward must use his judgment and decide quickly, and always pass slightly ahead of the player passed to.

When the time comes for shooting, the forward should not make straight for the goalkeeper, as then there will be but little room to shoot past him. A good cross shot is the best, and often, too, a shot with the outside of the foot will quite puzzle the goalkeeper, as he cannot tell to which side of the goal it is going. Some goalkeepers who are efficient at saving lofty shots will often fail at a low shot, and vice versa. Therefore, let the forward note his opportunity, and shoot according to circumstances. When the ball is near the opponents' goal it should be kept as much as possible to the three inner men. Much time is wasted by sending it out to the outside men, and at the same time it is almost impossible for them to shoot with success if the goalkeeper is of any use. When, however, the ball is centred, say, from the left wing, in my opinion the inside right should be about opposite to the right goalpost, and the outside right should not be more than eight or ten yards beyond him, which may give him a good chance of an easy cross shot. Backs and half-backs *must* be able to head, and a forward ought to be able to do so, but it is not nearly so necessary for him.

A great many forwards head too much in front of goal, and lose chance after chance, for it stands to reason that it is easier for a goalkeeper to save a shot that is in the air than to save a really fast low shot from the foot. Often I have seen a good middle hopelessly spoilt by the centre (though he could but touch the ball with a tuft of hair) turning it aside harmlessly to a back or the goalkeeper, or, more commonly, behind the goal line, when the forward beyond him would have had a clear shot. In conclusion, forwards should remember to 'hustle', that is, hamper, the opposing half-backs and backs, and endeavour to prevent them getting their kicks.

The advice of such a master of the art of attack as W. N. Cobbold will be thoroughly valued, even if it can only be fully appreciated by those who have acquired a certain amount of proficiency in the game, and have passed their 'little go' in the curriculum of football. In the ordinary way, a young player will learn more by practical experience and in emulating the style and tactics of really skilful opponents than in any amount of written instruction, however capable the writer.

The qualifications for a good forward have already been enumerated. Though in the main the same qualities are required in the case of each of the five forwards, there are, nonetheless, attributes that are more valuable in a centre than in a wing player, and vice versa. A centre, in particular, should be possessed of all the football virtues. He should have a certain amount of pace, but, more than all, he should be a strong as well as a safe kick, and with either foot, as well as a dead shot when near the opposite goal. As he has to do at times a lot of heavy work, and he is, as a rule, very carefully watched, particularly if he is of any exceptional capacity, he should be possessed of some weight. He is, to a great extent, the pivot on which the attack works, and his play, if he is above the average, is of infinite variety. When the ball is in the enemy's half, or at any distance from his own goal, his powers are less severely taxed, although he must always be the main or connecting link in the line of attack. In such cases he has, perhaps, better opportunities of setting in his own person an example of method and, at the same time, the advantages of combination. He should be on the alert to see in the simultaneous advance of the line which of the wings is in a better position when he is in danger of any serious obstruction himself, and directly he is likely to be stopped by one of the opposite side, he should pass out to the wing without the smallest hesitation.

There must, of course, be discretion as well as accuracy in the passing. Whether the exigencies of the situation should require this to be long or short, as a rule it is advisable to keep the ball low rather than lift it. High kicking is, indeed, under any circumstances likely to destroy its own object. In the case of a high wind it is not easy to do it to a nicety, and, moreover, if the ball is sent in the air, it gives the opposite backs a chance of getting to it and of heading it away. The changes in a game of football as it is now played, though, are so rapid that the whole secret of success is to gauge the precise merits of the opposition with a certain degree of accuracy, and to adopt the play of one's self and one's side to the exigencies of each situation as it arises.

I have given at some length the general requirements to form a really good centre. The inner wing players require, in a great measure, the same qualities, as their mission is, in the ordinary course, to feed the outside men, as well as to keep thoroughly in touch with the centre. The aim of all the forwards should of course be to have the line of the advance as complete as is possible. By this I mean that when one player has the ball, the others should be able to anticipate with some degree of certainty to whom he will pass, and the time at which such pass will be made. The latter will depend in a great measure on the positions of his own forwards, on the one hand, and on the other the amount of the opposition he is likely to meet on his way to the enemy's goal.

The player on the extreme outside, known as the outer wing, should be possessed of speed, for he often gets a chance of showing his pace, and very frequently a long pass out either from the centre or even the other side of the ground enables him to get well away almost without fear of opposition until he reaches the last line of defence. The fault of many of even the best outer wing players is to stick too long to the ball in the hope of getting ultimately well within range of the goalkeeper. As a rule, such delay is fatal, for it enables the enemy's back to return in time to cover their posts, and the attack is in every sense a failure. An experienced player would instead have foreseen this possibility, and have got rid of the ball to the centre before the opposite backs could have recovered their positions sufficiently to be able to hamper him. That side is the most dangerous in attack in which the passing shows the least hesitation. Precipitancy is as much to be avoided, but the judgment requisite to attain perfection in passing is sure to come with experience. Close dribbling is neat, and dodgy play naturally appeals to the gallery. It is 'magnificent, but it is not war', and forwards who affect this kind of game cannot be too soon displaced for others who are capable of grasping the great aim of the football strategist.

I have confined my remarks on the science of passing entirely to the forwards. It must not be forgotten, though, that the half-backs have something of the mission of the mounted infantry in military tactics. They have their value as offensive as well as defensive players, and, in fact, form a means of communication not only between the two wings, but between all the forwards in cases of urgency. The possibilities of forward play are too numerous to be dealt with in the limit of one chapter, and it will be sufficient for the purpose of this small volume to point out the chief essentials to completeness of combination.

One notable defect in many elevens, particularly in the South of England, is the want of attention shown by forwards in keeping off the opposite backs. The practice of obstructing – I mean legitimate obstruction, of course, by preventing him getting his kick – a back by one forward when another is making headway with the ball, is not as well carried out by many English teams as it should be. It ought to be a ruling principle, when the play is anywhere near the goal, for one or other of the forwards to impede and prevent the backs getting at the ball either by heading or kicking. Such tactics often demoralise the defence, and certainly destroy a great deal of its efficacy.

The same remark will apply with even greater force to the goalkeeper, who should be worried at every opportunity, so as to neutralise his efficiency as much as possible. The corner kick, in particular, should be utilised to this purpose, but, under any circumstances, the goalkeeper should, wherever it is practicable, be marked by the centre or one of the inner wing players, who should rush him so as to hinder him getting a chance of removing the ball.

It may appear superfluous to add that forwards should stick to their positions. The essence of combination is systematic working, and unless there is method, the forwards cannot be doing their duty. Each player should, indeed, as a general rule, shadow one of the opposite side, and this cannot be done unless each keeps fairly well to the position assigned to him. I have said already that passing along the ground is, in a great majority of cases, more likely to be of use than when the ball is sent to any height. The advantage is that it is mostly much easier to take the pass while in full swing. It may be accepted, too, as a general principle, that short passing will be of more real use than long, and, indeed, as a rule, it is only under special circumstances that the latter should be adopted.

# 8

# The Half-Backs

The defence, according to latter-day notions, is constituted of three half-backs, two full-backs, and a goalkeeper. A general principle as to the respective duties of each of the six players forming the rearguard has already been laid down. It is, however, the particular application to each individual case that remains to be supplied for the benefit of those who have not as yet graduated in the game. The addition of the third half-back was, in a great measure, to counteract the readiness of many forwards to take the fullest advantage of the opportunity of 'sneaking' allowed them by the offside rule, so long favoured by the lawbreakers of the Association, and, it must in fairness be added, accepted with approval by the great bulk of the players. The provision that keeps a man always onside as long as there are three between him and the opposite goal, offers undoubtedly a great temptation to forwards to get as far up as they can consistently with safety. To meet this, it was found necessary to strengthen the first line of defence, and the centre-half-back was introduced therefore, though his mission is, in a great measure, to feed the forwards, to enable the other halves to pay more attention, in fact to devote themselves mainly to stopping, or at least frustrating, the tactics of the opposite wing.

To be a really first-class half-back requires the possession of something more than skilful use of the feet. To fill the position well demands not only quickness of discernment to counteract the tactics of the opposite forwards, but also judgment and decision to be able to take advantage of the best opportunity to assist those of one's own side. The half-backs are, or ought to be, as useful for the purposes of attack as for defence. They need not necessarily be powerful, but it is essential that they should be quick, able to kick well with either foot as well as in any position and, at the same time, capable of heading should occasion require. They should obviously retreat or advance accordingly as the side has to attack or defend. If they are engaged in defensive tactics, they should on no account dribble, and, if they are hampered, it will be better rather to pass to one of the other halves or to give assistance to the backs, either by passing to them or by preventing any of the other side from interfering with the back or obstructing his kick. As a general rule, a half-back should not kick very hard. In defence he will often be of infinitely more use in worrying the opposite forwards, and checking them, than in kicking; in fact the backs are successful or unsuccessful in the majority of instances in proportion as the halves assist them by keeping off the opposite forwards.

If the halves have to take their part in the attack, their tactics will of course be of a different kind. In this case they have to assist the forwards, and the object is in the main to pass the ball to the player in the best position. Here, too, dribbling is unadvisable, though it is often practised to advantage. In passing to the forwards, the ball should be sent as low as possible, so as to give the least possible chance to the other side of meeting it. Passing of this kind is done with greater precision with the side of the foot, and indeed it will be found that it is much easier to attain accuracy in this way than with the point of the toe. Gallery kicking should be altogether discountenanced, and indeed the ability of a half-back is not in any way dependent on the extent of the work he does in this particular way. Opportunities occur, and not unfrequently, in a game where he has a good chance of a shot at goal, but, as a rule, his occupation consists chiefly in providing openings for others. He ought to be the mutual friend of the backs as well of the forwards – of equal assistance to the latter in defence as to the former in attack. At the same time, it must be remembered that they have to watch the opposite forwards carefully, and I had better add, in case I have omitted to lay any stress on it, that the centre-half-back should always keep the centre-forward of the opposite side well in his eye.

# 9

# The Full-Backs

The requirements for a full-back, though in some degree the same, are not altogether identical with those for a half-back. Here, again, it is necessary that there should be a thorough accord. The backs ought, indeed, to a great extent to act in harmony with the halves, and, as a matter of fact, the generally accepted theory is that the five players next in front of the goalkeeper should work in connection, or at least on a definite system of co-operation. The tactics of the back under any circumstances must be in the main dependent on those of the halves, and his policy will be guided generally by the movements of the halves, particularly of him directly in front. In the ordinary course he must watch his own half, i.e. on his own wing, or immediately before him if he happens to be in the centre. If the half-back goes at the opposite forward, and compels him to transfer the ball, the back will necessarily run in so as to get it before any other of the enemy's forwards can obtain the ball after such pass. Similar considerations will naturally influence the two backs, so that there may be the same mutual support by which in the event of the first going forward, the second may fall back to get the ball, if the other is, in football parlance, 'going for the man'.

Backs should not only be clever kicks, capable of taking the ball in any position and with either foot, but also be possessed of strength. They should never keep the ball by any chance a moment longer than is absolutely necessary, and it is needless therefore to add that they should never on any account be tempted to dribble. Backs, to be of real service too, require to exercise a great deal of judgment, as they have it in their power, by going forward on occasions, to keep the opposite forwards if they get too far up offside. Backs, moreover, have often to stand a good deal of the heavy work, and it is necessary therefore that they should have pluck as well as a certain amount of weight. As a general rule, when pressed they will find it expedient to send the ball well away to the wings. They must, too, not get so near the posts as to hamper or prevent the goalkeeper getting a good sight of the ball. The whole system of defence, though, is of such interest that it will be of great use if I give the views of perhaps the two greatest defensive players the game has produced – Messrs A. M. and P. M. Walters, incomparably the best pair of full-backs we have ever seen.

In discussing the defence, there are essentially two systems to which alone attention needs to be drawn. First, the independent, where every man acts for himself; secondly, the combined, or that system which recognises that prevention is better than cure. The independent system consists, as it were, of two ranks entirely separate from each other, in which the front rank, or, in other words, the half-backs, bear the brunt of the attack, and it is only when their defence is broken through that the backs are brought into action. This system obviously requires that the half-backs shall not only be first-rate players, but also in first-class condition, since not being assisted by the backs until the very last possible moment, they are in a minority of three to five, in addition to which as soon as they are passed they have to get back as quickly as they can.

In the combined system, on the other hand, there is no hard and fast line between backs and half-backs, though of course it can readily be understood that both backs must not be in an advanced position at the same time. Each man of the defence marks one forward of the opposite side, the backs and half-backs on each side respectively arranging between themselves which of them shall take the outside man, the centre-half acting rather more independently than the other two halves, but still paying more attention to the centre-forward than any of the others. As an illustration, suppose the ball to be run down the right wing of the attack, the left back and half of the defence will mark the two wing men, the right full-back will come across so as to be at hand to assist his fellow back, but keeping well behind in case the ball should be kicked beyond the left back and half. The centre-half will mark the centre-forward, and the right-half will take up such a position as will enable him to prevent either man of the left wing opposed to him taking a pass. This system distributes the work equally among the whole of the defence, and therefore requires less individual excellence, though utilising the powers of the full-backs to a far greater extent than the independent system. Each has its advantages, the former of the two alone answering when players are new to one another, and when the adoption of the latter would probably lead to disaster. The great advantages of the latter system where it can be adopted are:

1. It to a great extent prevents the opposing forwards getting the ball.
2. When by any chance they do get the ball, it prevents any combination whatever, as there is no clear space between the backs and half-backs in which they can get together.
3. It tends to put the opposing forwards offside, and so prevents 'lurking'.
4. It requires less individual excellence, and equalises the labour.

It is, perhaps, superfluous to add, nowadays, when the game is so well known, that neither halves nor full-backs should go in for gallery kicking, and least of all the halves. It is far easier, though less effective as a spectacle, to pass a ball back to a fellow back than to kick it over your own head. It should always be their object to place the ball to the forward who is in the best position for receiving it as conveniently for him to take as possible, that is, where feasible along the ground. To ensure accuracy, all passing by backs and half-backs to forwards should be done with the side of the foot; it looks twice as ugly as with the toe, but it is ten times more effective. Dribbling should never be indulged in beyond what is absolutely necessary, but passing from the half-back to backs, and also between the halves themselves, and between the backs themselves, is often extremely useful. Last, but by no means least important, where a half-back finds himself in such a position that he cannot reach the ball, or that it will be more easy for the back to do so, he must invariably *keep the man off.*

# 10

# The Goalkeeper

As the goalkeeper represents the last line of defence, it is imperative that he should be a safe man. He should be cool in an emergency, ready witted, with plenty of pluck and unlimited go. Though it is a great advantage for him to be an adept in kicking with either foot, as a general rule he should use his hands to stop, even if he has time to get rid of the ball with his feet He should be strong enough to withstand a heavy charge, for he has every chance of being severely hustled if the opposite forwards are thoroughly up to their work. It is distinctly bad play to put the ball back even under the most critical circumstances in front of the goal; however hard he should be pressed, he ought always to make a point of relieving his goal by getting the ball away towards the wings, where it is, comparatively at least, out of danger. It is a very risky proceeding, too, to get even a few yards from the posts, as the game is so fast that his goal may be carried before he is able to return. It is always advisable to use both hands whenever possible in stopping the ball, and fisting out should be discouraged except when there is real necessity. It is undoubtedly an advantage for a goalkeeper to be a strong kick, as where the kick-off from behind has to be taken at all frequently the backs are thereby spared a lot of heavy work, and are thus able to be of very much greater use to the side.

In the event of a free-kick or throw in from touch near the goal line, or a corner kick, the goalkeeper should not be hampered by the backs, but allowed plenty of room and a good sight of the ball. This is of urgent importance, as any restriction of his freedom at such times prevents him following the ball closely, and where the smallest hesitation is fatal, he should have nothing to interfere with his view of the ball.

Practice will alone make a really expert goalkeeper. Judgment, as well as activity and dexterity, are essential for a thorough fulfilment of the duties of the position, and this is a combination of qualities not easily obtainable.

*Above:* An anxious time near goal.

*Below:* The Wolves were no match for Preston in the 1889 FA Cup final, winning 3-0.

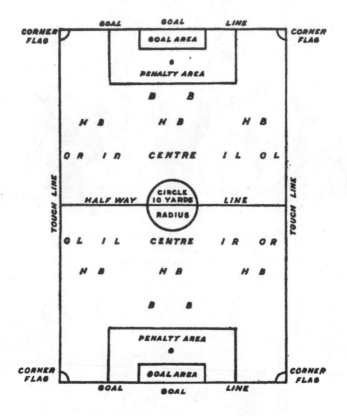

Plan of the field of play – referred to in the law of the game.
B: back; HB: half-back; OL: outside left; IL: inside left; OR:
outside right; IR: inside right.

*Above:* Champions of the Sheffield Challenge Cup in 1891. Back row: Cuthbert, Mr J. Le Brun (committee), Massey, McDonald (trainer), Grey, Mr W. Reid (committee), Parr, James, Mr J. Musson (secretary), Pilkington. Front row: Kisby, McCullum, Langton, Herod, Oresham. (*Courtesy of Jason Dickinson*).

*Below:* Preston beat WBA 1-0 in the 1889 FA Cup semi-final.

JUST OVER THE BAR. SAVED !

*Above:* A goalkeeper just tips the ball over the crossbar.

*Left:* John Goodall, centre-forward for England and Preston North End.

WELL SAVED! A HOT SHOT STOPPED.

*Above:* The goalkeeper was quick to save this cross.

*Right:* Harry Butler Daft won the FA Cup as part of the Notts County team in 1894.

WEDNESDAY AT PLAY

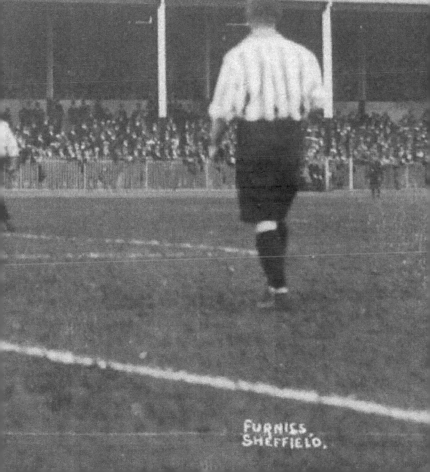

FURNISS, SHEFFIELD.

*Above:* Tripping was originally allowed in football when the player was running with the ball.

*Below:* The last line of defence, the goalkeeper must be able to stand up under extreme pressure.

WELL KICKED! JUST TOO LATE.

*Above:* A scramble in front of goal. (*Courtesty of Jason Dickinson*)

*Right:* Despite being only 5 foot 5, William Bassett played 261 Football League games for West Bromwich Albion, scoring 61 goals, and he won 16 England caps (scoring 8 goals). He was one of the game's earliest celebrities.

*Above:* A shot goes wide during an early Football League game.

*Below:* Holding, tripping and hacking all used to be legal in the early football matches, making the game a lot more dangerous than today's version.

*Above:* A system of co-operation must exist between the forwards to make a successful and winning team.

*Right:* James Trainer was for several years the best goalkeeper of the Football League. He earned the moniker in the 1888/89 season when he was part of the unbeaten Preston North End team, nicknamed 'The Invincibles'.

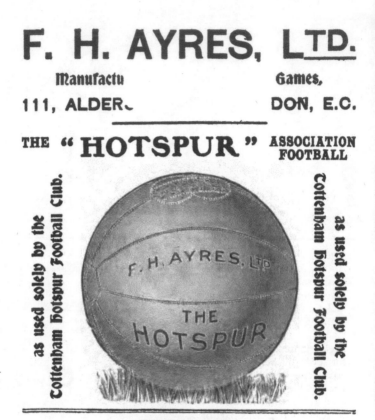

# 11

# General Hints

I have endeavoured to represent, as concisely as possible, the essentials for the acquirement of any great degree of excellence in any of the positions that constitute the formation of a football team. There are, however, some general rules that must be carried out strictly if the game is to be conducted in a spirit of true sport. They are so obvious that it might appear superfluous in a work of this character to give them any prominence. Yet they are in the case of even experienced players, who ought to set a better example, very often overlooked, or, in the excitement of the moment, forgotten.

The power of a captain, as I have said in an earlier chapter, must be absolute. It is he who should make any appeals that may be required, and, though this is not always an infallible test, his capacity to command in the ordinary way may be gauged by the discipline of the team. A good captain will do his spiriting gently. His control of his men is as often as possible the result of the force of his own example, and, like Harry Coverdale, a capable captain has generally a quiet way of settling things, which is effective by the very reason of it.

Football must always, in a measure, be attended with a certain amount of risks. It is this spice of danger that makes it so essentially English, and gives it a high place among our national sports.

For this very reason, though, it should be the aim of every player to discountenance, and earnestly, anything like intentional roughness. Charging is at times, of course, necessary, but there can be moderation even in this. Tricky tactics are infinitely more conducive to accident, and of late, particularly among northern players, there has been a growing tendency to stoop to trip, or to take other unfair advantages, which, even if they do not actually come within the scope of the law, should be checked with a very high hand. Football will inevitably suffer, and materially, in public favour if the standard of it is lowered, as it will undoubtedly be if those who have the control of clubs do not fearlessly uphold a spirit of manliness and insist on the discouragement of any questionable practices with a view of getting a momentary advantage. The future of football emphatically depends on the firmness of those in authority, and even the merely reckless player should be taught that he is doing an injury to the game, and the incorrigible offender be punished without mercy.

It ought to be a cardinal sin to interfere in any way with the officials. Linesmen and referees are not infallible, and modern football is so fast that it is at times quite impossible for the most active of them to keep up with the ball throughout a hard game. The very fact of their appointment, though, ought to ensure that they are treated with respect. In many cases, the referee's position, it must be admitted, is anything but an enviable one, and where local excitement runs high his is a thankless task. The general tendency of recent legislation, however, has been to arm him with increased powers to deal with rough play, and if he exercises them without fear he can minimise it to a great extent. It might appear to be unnecessary even to hint that the decision of a referee should be, under any circumstances, accepted without a question. On all matters of fact his verdict is final and subject to no appeal. A practised and capable official will give his decision promptly and unhesitatingly, and will not, as some of the less experienced sometimes do, argue the point, or assign the reasons that have influenced him in giving his verdict. In any case, whatever disputes may arise, the captain should alone be the spokesman of the side.

It cannot be too clearly pointed out, too, that the referee is not infallible. His position, at the same time, is one of the greatest responsibility, and his authority is, as it ought to be, paramount. He has, for instance, power to stop the game whenever he may think fit – by reason of darkness, interference of spectators, or other cause, either permanently or for such a time as he may think fit, whenever he may deem such a course necessary. In addition, he has the right to award a free-kick without any appeal in a case where he thinks the conduct of a player is dangerous, or likely to prove dangerous.

If the young player has in him a natural instinct for the game, he ought to derive benefit from a careful study of the advice given in this work. There are some points, though, in the rules that often cause misapprehension, and it will perhaps be of use if some of them are dealt with. A few years since the committee of the Football Association issued some memoranda for the guidance of officials, and as these embrace the various questions about which there is often a difference of opinion among the ill-informed, they may be utilised for the general good of players as well as officials.

The kick-off must be in the direction of the opposite goal line. It is not allowable to start the ball towards your own line, and while the opposite side shall not approach within ten yards of the ball till it is kicked off, no one shall pass the centre of the ground towards the opposite goal till it has been started. A goal is won when the ball has *passed* between the goalposts – ergo, the whole must go over the line to produce a score. In the same way the ball must go completely over the touchline to be out of play, and it must not necessarily touch the ground before it is out of play.

The offside rule is a source of much trouble to players who will not take ordinary pains to master its special features. A player cannot be offside unless he is in front of the ball, and then only if less than three of the other side are between him and the opposite goal. It is the fact of being *in front* of the ball, and kicked by one of his own men too, which tends to make one offside and he cannot be offside if the ball was last played (i.e. touched, kicked, or thrown) by one of his own side who *at the time of kicking* is nearer his opponents' goal than himself. The stumbling is often in the words just marked with italics. The time of the kick constitutes the time of the infringement of the rule. A player who has less than three of the opposite side in front when the ball is sent from behind him by one of his own side is offside *at the time of kicking,* and cannot put himself onside until the ball has been played by one of his opponents. Nor can he obstruct one of the enemy to prevent him taking his kick, or in any way whatever interfere with any other player.

A goalkeeper is allowed to use his hands *in defence of his goal*; i.e. in his own half of the ground, and he may not be charged except when he is holding the ball, or obstructing an opponent, or when he has passed outside the goal area.

Players wearing nails, bars or studs on their boots, other than as provided in the rules, it is enacted 'shall be prohibited from taking further part in the match' and in the common interests of the players, and with a view to minimise the risks of the game, this power should be firmly exercised.

A ball touching a linesman or referee is not dead.

Players should remember that a ball is always in play after an appeal until a decision is given by the referee.

Handling is strictly forbidden to any one but the goalkeeper, and under the reservations above stated. Handling is *wilfully* playing the ball with the hand or arm. The interpretation of *wilful*, of course, rests with the referee. The referee has also the power where a player is intentionally tripped, charged from behind, held or pushed by an opponent within twelve yards from the opposite goal line, to give a penalty kick.

The penalty kick, which was introduced in the season of 1891/92, has been a source of great anxiety to those who have to make the laws. It is the punishment for *intentional* infringement of Law 9 *by the defending side within the penalty area*. Rule 9 proscribes tripping, kicking, or jumping at a player, intentionally handling the ball, holding or pushing an opponent, or charging an opponent violently or dangerously, or charging from behind unless the player charged is intentionally obstructing an opponent In other breaches of the rules, the outcome is a free-kick. In the latter case the free-kick has to be taken from the place where the offence occurred, and no players of the opposing side are allowed to approach within six yards of the ball unless the ball is within six yards of the goal line, behind which players are not required to stand. It is to be regretted, of course, that a condition of things should have arisen to make such a severely repressive measure as the penalty kick advisable. At the same time one is bound to admit that it has proved to be a necessity, and as its importance cannot be overrated, it looms largely in any outline of the actual play.

# 12

# Rules of the Football Association Ltd

These Rules must be read in conjunction with the Articles of Association (see Article 49). Many of the provisions previously contained in the Rules are now embodied in the Articles, and are not therefore repeated in these Rules.

The decisions of the Council are printed as notes at the foot of the page.

1. The Association shall consist of such Clubs and Associations playing Association Football and being otherwise qualified according to the Laws, Rules, Regulations and Byelaws of the Association as the Council may approve.

2. In the interpretation of these Rules the words 'The Football Association', 'The Association', or 'This Association', mean 'The Football Association Limited', except where the context requires a different meaning.

3. All Clubs, before being affiliated to the Association, shall satisfy the Council that they are properly constituted Clubs, and playing football according to the Laws of the Association.

   Each Club shall forward to the Secretary on or before the first day of October in each year, a return in accordance with form A.

A Club shall not withdraw its membership from an Affiliated Association without the consent of this Association.

Except as provided by Rule 4, no Club shall be affiliated to this Association unless it has been in existence for at least two years immediately previous to application being made for affiliation, and has during that period been a member of its County or District Affiliated Association if the Rules of such Association permit. No application for affiliation shall be made between the first day of March and the first day of August in each year. A Club shall cease to be a member of this Association when it ceases to be a member of its County or District Affiliated Association, but this condition shall not apply to a Club that was a member of this Association on the first day of May 1899, and which was not at that date a member of its County or District Affiliated Association, nor to a Professional Club within the area of an Association, the Rules of which do not permit of the affiliation of Professional Clubs.

4. A Professional Club within the area of an Association, the rules of which do not permit of the affiliation of Professional Clubs, may affiliate to this Association, but a Club so affiliated shall not be entitled to representation or voting power until full membership has been granted by the Council under Rule 3.

5. All Associations before being affiliated to the Association shall consist of properly constituted Clubs. Each Association shall cover a defined area, and shall neither extend

nor alter such area without having obtained the consent of the Council. Each Association shall forward to the Secretary on or before the first day of November in each year, a return in accordance with form B.

6. The Subscription for each affiliated Association or Club shall be 10s 6d per annum (payable during the first week in May, or within one week after joining), with an entrance fee of 10s 6d. The Council shall have the power to admit any Foreign or Colonial Associations or Clubs as members of this Association on payment of an Annual Subscription of 5s. Such Foreign or Colonial Associations or Clubs shall not be entitled to send any representative to the Council. An Association or Club whose subscription is unpaid on the first day of August shall cease to be a member of this Association.

7. The Annual General meeting shall be held between the 20th and the 31st of May in each year. The Secretary shall give seven clear days' notice to all affiliated Associations and Clubs of the place, the day and the hour of such Meeting. A printed abstract of the Treasurer's accounts and an agenda specifying the nature of the business to be transacted at that Meeting shall accompany the notice.

8. The names of the proposed Officers and Auditors, with the names of their proposers and seconders, shall be sent to the Secretary on or before the 1st day of May in each year.

9. Notice of any business (other than the Election of Officers, appointing Auditors,

and the consideration of the Accounts and Balance Sheet, and of the Report of the Council, and not being such as by Statute requires a special resolution) to be submitted at the Annual General Meeting, shall be given to the Secretary on or before the 1st day of May in each year, and a copy of such notice, with the names of the proposer and seconder, shall be sent to the affiliated Associations and Clubs on or before the 8th day of May in each year. Notice of any amendment to the business to be so submitted shall be given to the Secretary on or before the 15th day of May in each year.

10. The Secretary shall convene an Extraordinary General Meeting at any time on receiving a requisition stating the objects of the Meeting and signed by the Secretaries of not less than twenty Associations or Clubs affiliated to this Association. The Council have power at any time to convene a Special General Meeting for the purpose of submitting to the Meeting any alterations or additions to these Rules that the Council may deem expedient. An agenda of the business to be transacted at any such Meeting (or at any Extraordinary General Meeting convened by the Council under Article 20) shall accompany the notice convening the Meeting.

11. The Association shall be governed by a Council, consisting of the officers (i.e. a President, six Vice-Presidents, and a Treasurer), ten representatives

of Divisions, and representatives from affiliated Associations, all of whom shall be duly qualified according to the Articles and Rules, and elected annually as therein provided. The retiring Council shall be eligible for re-election. The representatives of Divisions and Associations shall retire on the 30th day of June in each year. All past Presidents of the Association shall *ex officio* be members of the Council and entitled to vote.

12. Each Association that has been affiliated to this Association for the last three years, and has fifty or more Clubs that have been members thereof for at least one year, shall be entitled to send a representative to the Council, who must be elected as herein provided, and shall not be changed except by previous consent of the Council. Every Association claiming to return a representative to the Council, shall, during the month of June in each year, forward the name and address of such representative to the Secretary, together with a return in accordance with form C. Where Associations overlap each other, the senior Association shall have jurisdiction over a Club that is a member of that and another Association. The Secretary, on ascertaining the correctness of the claims, shall declare such representative duly elected. Any subsequent claims shall be submitted to the Council. The Clubs playing Association Football at the Universities of Oxford and Cambridge shall collectively be deemed to be Associations within these Rules, and

each University Association shall be entitled annually to appoint a Representative to the Council, but such Representative may not be changed during the year, except with the previous consent of the Council. The Council shall have power annually to elect to the Council a Representative of the Public School Clubs of the country.

13. The Secretary shall, immediately after the meeting held according to Article 42, send a form of nomination, with a list of all the Divisions and the Clubs composing them, to each Club belonging to this Association, and such form shall be duly filled up and returned to the Secretary on or before a date to be therein named (not being less than seven nor more than fourteen days after the date upon which the same shall be so sent by the Secretary).

14. Every candidate shall be nominated by three Clubs on form F. Such nomination shall be signed by the Chairman and Secretary of the Committee of each Club for and on behalf of their Clubs. If only one candidate is nominated for a division, the Secretary shall declare him elected. If more than one candidate is nominated for any division the Secretary shall forthwith, after the time fixed for the close of the nominations, send a list of the candidates nominated and a form of voting paper to each Club in every such division, and such voting paper shall be duly filled up and returned to the Secretary on or before a date to be therein named (not being less than three nor more than six days after the date upon which

the same shall be so sent by the Secretary). Every such voting paper shall be marked on the outside, 'Voting Paper', and shall be opened only by the Returning Officer or his Deputy. The President shall be the Returning Officer, and he may appoint a Deputy.

15. The Returning Officer shall, immediately after the date fixed for the return of Voting Papers, open and examine such Voting Papers. The candidate for each Division receiving the greatest number of votes shall be declared duly elected. If there is a tie, the election shall be determined by a vote of the members present at the first meeting of such members of the Council as shall have been duly elected. Where there are more than two candidates for any Division, unless one candidate has an absolute majority of Clubs in the division, the candidate receiving the least number of votes shall retire. The division shall be polled again, until there is either an absolute majority or a tie.

16. A candidate shall not, neither shall any person on behalf of any candidate, offer any bribe, consideration, or other improper inducement to any Club for the purpose of procuring the vote of the said Club in the election of such candidate to the Council. Breach of this Rule shall be deemed serious misconduct. In addition to any other penalty that the Council may deem fit to impose, this offence shall render void the election of such candidate, if he shall have been elected a member of the Council.

17. In case of an objection to any election the Council may order a new election, or fill up a vacancy instead of ordering a new election if they shall think proper.

18. If in any Division no candidate is nominated, the Secretary shall report the circumstance to the Council, who may fill the vacancy.

19. The Council shall keep three separate accounts: (1) The International Match Account, which shall contain all receipts and payments in connection with the International Matches; (2) The Investment Account, containing all receipts and payments in connection with the Interest, Dividends and Investments of the Association; (3) The General Account, being all the other receipts and payments of the Association. If any dispute arises as to the apportionment of any item to a particular account, the Council shall settle such dispute, and their decision shall be final.

20. The Council may each year appropriate such part of the monies standing to the credit of the International Match Account, or the Investment Account, as they may deem necessary, for the purposes of a Benevolent Fund, and may distribute the monies so appropriated among necessitous players and others who have rendered service to the game.

21. For the transaction of business at a Council Meeting, five members shall form a quorum. The Council may fill any vacancy that occurs in their body, appoint a Secretary and such other assistance as they think fit, appoint

such Committees or Commissions as they may consider necessary, delegate all or any of their powers to any such Committee or Commission of the Council, or to any affiliated Association or Associations, and make such regulations for the management of the Association and control of the game as from time to time may be necessary. Resolutions and decisions of the Council shall be binding upon all affiliated Associations and Clubs and all members thereof, until they are rescinded or varied by the vote of a majority present and voting at a General Meeting.

22  Associations, Leagues or other Combinations of Clubs shall not be formed without the consent of this Association, or of an affiliated Association. All applications for formation shall be made on form D. All Associations, Leagues or other Combinations of Clubs shall observe the Rules, Regulations and By-laws of this Association. Associations or Clubs belonging to this or an affiliated Association shall not play against any Association or Club belonging to any Association, League or Combination of Clubs to which such consent has not been given.

23. Charity Associations or Benefit Competitions shall not be formed without the consent of this Association or of an affiliated Association. All applications for formation shall be made on form E. All Charity Associations or Benefit Competitions shall observe the Rules, Regulations and By-laws of this Association.

Associations or Clubs belonging to this or an affiliated Association shall not play or take part in any Charity Association or Benefit Competition to which consent has not been given.

24 This Association, or any affiliated Association, shall have power to prohibit the Clubs under its jurisdiction from playing with or against any Club that is not a member of this or any affiliated Association.

25. Clubs and players shall not compete in any match or competition, the proceeds of which are not devoted to a recognised Football Club or Football Association or some other object approved of by this or by an affiliated Association. Six-a-side and similar irregular competitions at which gate money is taken are forbidden, unless the consent of the local affiliated Association has been obtained. Where two affiliated Associations cover the same area, the permission must be obtained from the senior Association.

26. Matches shall not be played on Sundays within the jurisdiction of this Association. A player shall not be compelled to play on Sundays outside the jurisdiction of this Association. A Club shall not be compelled to play any match on Good Friday or Christmas Day.

27. Matches are prohibited during the close season, which commences on the 1st May and ends on the 31st August in each year. After the 15th August, practice matches may be played between teams of the same Club, and professionals who have not been

engaged for the following season may be given a trial by any Club. Except for some institution approved by this or an affiliated Association, gate money must not be taken at practice matches in the close season. Army and Navy teams, and teams of the Auxiliary Forces, may play in competitions in the close season while in camp, and registered players may take part therein. The competitions shall be strictly confined to the units concerned, and gate money must not be taken.

28. Clubs shall not play matches with Scratch Teams, when any consideration is paid to the Scratch Teams or anyone connected therewith, without the permission of this Association or of the local affiliated Association. Two Scratch Teams shall not play against each other when gate money is taken without the permission of this Association, or of the local affiliated Association in whose district the match takes place. Where two affiliated Associations cover the same area the permission must be obtained from the senior Association.

29. Players are either amateur or professional. Any player registered with this Association as a professional, or receiving remuneration or consideration of any sort above his necessary hotel and travelling expenses actually paid, shall be considered to be a professional. Training expenses not paid by the players themselves will be considered as remuneration beyond necessary travelling and hotel expenses. Amateur players receiving any payment must give

a written receipt for the same, stating particulars of expenses, and secretaries must produce such receipt to the Council of this Association at any time if required to do so. If an amateur player is engaged by a Club in any capacity for which he receives remuneration, the Club may be required to prove, to the satisfaction of the Association, that his services as a player do not affect the amount of remuneration paid to him. Players competing for any money prizes in football contests shall be considered professionals. When a player is registered as a professional, he at once loses his status as an amateur. When an amateur player is injured while playing football, he shall, upon obtaining the consent of this Association, or the local affiliated Association, be entitled to receive his doctor's fees, or the proceeds of any benefit match, subscription or collection, without losing his amateur status. Where two affiliated Associations cover the same area, the permission must be obtained from the senior Association.

30. Every professional shall be registered on form G. Each form, after all particulars have been filled in, including the date of signature, must be signed by the professional (his signature being attested), and returned to the Secretary of this Association within five days of such signature. Except as provided by Rule 27, a professional shall not be allowed to play until this Rule has been complied with, and the Secretary of the Club registering the player shall have

received the acknowledgment on the official form from the Secretary of this Association. Players may be transferred from one Club to another (see Form H). A club shall not be allowed to register a professional unless he is a member of this Association, or an affiliated Association. After the 1 January 1908, no Club shall be entitled to pay or receive any transfer fee or other payment exceeding £350 upon or in respect of the transfer of any player.

31. The registration of professionals shall be binding for only one season, except as otherwise provided by these Rules, but a professional may during the month of April register himself for the following season for his own Club, but shall not enter into any engagement with another Club until his existing engagement has terminated. Until the period of registration of a professional player has expired he shall not be approached by any other Club, or an official of any other Club, or any other person, with the view to induce him to leave the Club for which he is registered when his engagement has terminated. No payment shall be made to Commission Agents or other persons than Clubs and players concerned in transfers and engagements of players. Clubs shall be entitled to retain players to whom they are prepared to pay the maximum wages, unless the players satisfy the Council that there are special grounds for allowing them to change their club.

32. Clubs shall not pay any Player a bonus of more than £4 as a consideration for

his signing a professional form. A bonus cannot be paid to a player on his re-signing for his own Club. The maximum wages that may be paid to any player shall be £4 per week or £208 per annum, but this restriction shall not apply to any payment made by this Association in respect of any of its matches. The payment of bonuses dependent on the result of any match shall not be allowed. A player may be allowed a benefit (1) after five years' service with a Club, (2) in case of accident or illness, or (3) when he is giving up playing. A player shall not be entitled to a second benefit within five years of the previous benefit. The consent of the Council of this Association must be obtained before a player is promised or receives a benefit.

33. The Council shall, subject to these Rules, have power to cancel the registration of a professional at any time upon application of the player, or of his Club, or may transfer him from one Club to another. A professional transferred must be re-registered by the Club to which he is transferred. The Council shall also have power to reinstate as an amateur any professional. All applications for reinstatement must be made on the Form to be supplied by the Secretary of this Association marked K in the Schedule annexed to these Rules, and, except in the case of a professional joining the Army, must be sent to the Secretary between the 1st and 31st of May in each year, and the Council will decide upon the same. A professional joining the Army may

be reinstated immediately on application, but shall not be again registered as a professional until the expiration of two years from the date of his reinstatement; neither, during that period, shall he play as an amateur for any Club except an Army Club.

34. All agreements between Clubs and professional players must be in writing and signed within seven days of the player signing the registration form. Except by mutual consent, no Club or player shall be entitled to determine the agreement between them during a current season without the consent of the Council of this Association. Agreements may provide that a player shall only be paid when played in matches, but if any such player is not played for a period of one month, he shall be at liberty to apply to this Association for the cancellation of the Agreement without conditions.

35. Except as provided by Rule 27, a professional player shall only play for the Club by which he is registered without the special permission of this Association.

36. Any League or other combination of Clubs sanctioned by this Association may provide in its Rules for a system whereby a player registered with such League or Combination may be retained, or a transfer fee demanded after the end of a season's engagement. If such provision is made, the Rules of any such League or Combination must provide that a player, if professional, cannot be retained at the end of the season without payment of wages, or the offer of

reasonable terms of reengagement, or if amateur, without being played regularly. Any player unable to agree upon terms of reengagement or transfer with the Club by which he is registered, shall have a right of, and must, in the first instance, appeal to the Committee of Management of the League or Combination to which such Club is attached. Every League or Combination must, if this Association so requires it, annually elect a Board of Appeal consisting (1) in the case of Leagues or Combinations operating in areas controlled by more than one County or District Association, of three Members of the Council of this Association, or (2) where the Clubs comprising such League or Combination are all within the area of the same County or District Association, of three Members of the Committee of that County or District Association. The Members forming the Boards of Appeal elected by the various Leagues or Combinations must in all cases be approved by the Council of this Association. Any appeal as to terms of reengagement or transfer as aforesaid from the decision of a Management Committee must be to the Board of Appeal, but no appeal shall be entertained unless the Board of Appeal is satisfied that the decision of the Committee of Management is contrary to the Rules of such League or Combination as sanctioned by the Council of this Association.

37. A professional shall not be allowed to serve on the Council of this Association, or on the Committee of any Association, League,

or Club, or represent his own or any other Association, League, or Club at any football meeting. When any person gives notice in writing to the Secretary of this Association that he has ceased to play football, the Council may, if they think fit, exempt such person from the operation of this Rule.

38. An amateur player may in writing intimate to the Secretary of this Association the Clubs for which he is a playing member, and lists shall be published. Without at least forty-eight hours' notice to the Clubs of which he is a member, no Club or Official of any Club shall induce or attempt to induce a bona fide player of any Club to become a professional, or leave his club until the end of the current season. A bona fide player is one who has played for his club during the current season or who has intimated to the Secretary of the Association as provided by this Rule.

39. An amateur player may be insured by his Club against accidents that occur during play. The insurance must be effected with a recognised Assurance Company.

40. In International Matches the qualification shall be birth. In the case of British subjects born abroad, their nationality shall be decided by the nationality of their fathers. In County and District Association Matches a player may only represent one County Association and one District Association in the same season, and he must be a bona fide member of a Club belonging to the County or District Association for which he plays.

41. The knickerbockers worn by players must be long enough to reach the knee.

42. Players, officials and spectators are only allowed to take part in or attend matches on condition that they observe the Rules, Regulations, and By-laws of this Association, and every affiliated Association or Club is required to observe and enforce such Rules, Regulations and By-laws.

43. Every Association or Club is responsible to the Council for the action of its players, officials, and spectators, and is required to take all precautions necessary to prevent spectators threatening or assaulting officials and players during or at the conclusion of matches. No official of an Association or Club, Referee, Linesmen or player shall bet on any Football Match, and Associations and Clubs are also required to prevent betting and the use of objectionable language by spectators. In the case of a breach of this Rule, any player, official, or spectator may be removed from any ground, and such force used as may be necessary for the purpose of effecting such a removal.

44. Associations affiliated to this Association shall have the power to deal with violations of the Laws of the Game, the Rules, Regulations and By-laws of this Association, or misconduct, by any of their Clubs or Associations that are not directly affiliated to this Association, or by any of their players, officials or members.

45. In the event of any Association, Club, player, official, member or spectator being

proved to the satisfaction of the Council to have been guilty of any violations of the Laws of the Game, the Rules, Regulations, and By-laws of this Association, or of any misconduct, the Council shall have the power to order the offending Association, Club, player, official, member or spectator to be removed from this Association, suspended for a stated period, or dealt with in such a manner as the Council may think fit. Any Association, Club, or player playing with or against the offending Association, Club or player after such removal, or during such time of suspension, shall also be dealt with in such manner as the Council may think fit. No suspended player or member of any Association or Club so suspended or removed from this Association shall be eligible for membership of any other Association or Club belonging to this Association without the special permission of the Council. The Council may also order offending Clubs to pay all expenses incurred in hearing the case.

46. The Association shall be entitled to publish in the public press, or in any other manner it shall think fit, reports of its proceedings, acts and resolutions, whether the same shall or shall not reflect on the character or conduct of any club, official, player or spectator, and every such club, official, player, or spectator shall be deemed to have assented to such publication.

47. Appeals from the decisions of Affiliated Associations may be made to the Council, but the operation of such decisions shall

not be suspended pending the hearing of an appeal unless the Council so order. Every appeal under this rule must be accompanied by a deposit of £10. On the hearing of the appeal the Council shall have power to vary, reverse, reduce or increase the penalty imposed by the Affiliated Association. No appeal shall be entertained unless the Council is satisfied that the decision of the Affiliated Association is contrary to the principles and practice of this Association and the Football Association heretofore.

48. The Council may call upon the Clubs, Associations or individuals charged with offending against the Rules, to prove to the satisfaction of the Council that the offence has not been committed, and failing such satisfactory proof the Clubs or individuals may be adjudged guilty of the offence. The Council shall have power to call upon any Associations, Clubs or players to produce any books, letters or documents, and other evidence the Council may desire.

49. Any complaint or claim made by a Club or player shall be in writing, and duplicate copies shall be sent to the Secretary accompanied by a deposit of twenty shillings, which deposit shall be forfeited if the complaint be not sustained. In the event of a frivolous or vexatious complaint being made, the Council shall have power to compel the complaining Club or player to pay such expenses of the Club or player complained of as may be deemed fit. Any complaint relating to the non-fulfilment of a match fixture, or claim under guarantee,

must be made within twenty-eight days from the date upon which the match was played or should have been played. Neither barrister nor solicitor shall represent a Club or player at the hearing of a complaint or claim unless he be the Secretary of the Club concerned, and appear as such in the printed list of secretaries in the official rule book.

50. Any player selected to play in any International or other match arranged by this Association and (without good and sufficient cause) refusing to comply with the arrangements of the Council for playing the match, or failing to play in such match, may be adjudged by the Council to have been guilty of misconduct, and any Club who may be deemed to have encouraged or instigated such player to commit a breach of instruction or rule, shall be deemed guilty of a similar offence.

## The Football Association Laws of the Game

1. The game should be played by eleven players on each side. The field of play shall be as shown in the plan subject to the following provisions: the dimensions of the field of play shall be maximum length, 130 yards; minimum length, 100 yards; maximum breadth, 100 yards; minimum breadth, 50 yards. The field of play shall be marked by boundary lines. The lines at each end are the goal lines, and the lines at the sides are the touch lines. The touch lines shall be drawn at right angles with the

goal lines. A flag with a staff not less than 5 feet high shall be placed at each corner. A halfway line shall be marked out across the field of play. The centre of the field of play shall be indicated by a suitable mark, and a circle with a 10-yards radius shall be made round it. The goals shall be upright posts fixed on the goal lines, equidistant from the corner flagstaffs, 8 yards apart, with a bar across them 8 feet from the ground. The maximum width of the goalposts and the maximum depth of the crossbar shall be 5 inches. Lines shall be marked 0 yards from each goalpost at right angles to the goal lines for a distance of 6 yards, and these shall be connected with each other by a line parallel to the goal lines; the space within these lines shall be the goal area. Lines shall be marked 18 yards from each goalpost at right angles to the goal lines for a distance of 18 yards, and these shall be connected with each other by a line parallel to the goal lines; the space within these lines shall be the penalty area. A suitable mark shall be made opposite the centre of each goal, 12 yards from the goal line; this shall be the penalty kick mark. The circumference of the ball shall not be less than 27 inches nor more than 28 inches. The outer casing of the ball must be of leather, and no material shall be used in the construction of the ball that would constitute a danger to the players. In International matches, the dimensions of the field of play shall be maximum length, 120 yards; minimum length, 110 yards; minimum breadth, 70 yards; and at the commencement of the game the weight of the ball shall be from 13 to 15 ounces.

2. The duration of the game shall be 90 minutes, unless otherwise mutually agreed upon. The winners of the toss shall have the option of kick-off or choice of goals. The game shall be commenced by a place kick from the centre of the field of play in the direction of the opponents' goal line; the opponents shall not approach within 10 yards of the ball until it is kicked off, nor shall any player on either side pass the centre of the ground in the direction of his opponents' goal until the ball is kicked off.

3. Ends shall only be changed at half-time. The interval at half-time shall not exceed five minutes, except by consent of the Referee. After a goal is scored the losing side shall kick-off, and after the change of ends at half-time the ball shall be kicked off by the opposite side from that which originally did so; and always as provided in Law 2.

4. Except as otherwise provided by these Laws, a goal shall be scored when the ball has passed between the goalposts under the bar, not being thrown, knocked on, nor carried by any player of the attacking side. If from any cause during the progress of the game the bar is displaced, the Referee shall have power to award a goal if in his opinion the ball would have passed under the bar if it had not been displaced. The ball is in play if it rebounds from a goalpost, crossbar, or a corner flagstaff into the field

of play. The ball is in play if it touches the Referee or a Linesman when in the field of play. The ball is out of play when it has crossed the goal line or touch line, either on the ground or in the air.

5. When the ball is in touch, a player of the opposite side to that which played it out shall throw it in from the point on the touch line where it left the field of play. The player throwing the ball must stand on the touch line facing the field of play, and shall throw the ball in over his head with both hands in any direction, and it shall be in play when thrown in. A goal shall not be scored from a throw-in, and the thrower shall not again play until the ball has been played by another player. This Law is complied with if the player has any part of both feet on the line when he throws the ball in.

6. When a player plays the ball, or throws it in from touch, any player of the same side who at such moment of playing or throwing in is nearer to his opponents' goal line is out of play, and may not touch the ball himself, nor in any way whatever interfere with an opponent, or with the play, until the ball has been again played, unless there are at such moment of playing or throwing in at least three of his opponents nearer their own goal line. A player is not out of play in the case of a corner kick, or when the ball is kicked off from goal, or when it has been last played by an opponent.

7. When the ball is played behind the goal line by a player of the opposite side, it shall

be kicked off by any one of the players behind whose goal line it went, within that half of the goal nearest the point where the ball left the field of play; but, if played behind by any one of the side whose goal line it is, a player of the opposite side shall kick it from within 1 yard of the nearest corner flagstaff. In either case an opponent shall not be allowed within 6 yards of the ball until it is kicked off.

8. The goalkeeper may, within his own half of the field of play, use his hands, but shall not carry the ball. The goalkeeper shall not be charged except when he is holding the ball, or obstructing an opponent, or when he has passed outside the goal area. The goalkeeper may be changed during the game, but notice of such change must first be given to the Referee.

9. Neither tripping, kicking, nor jumping at a player shall be allowed. A player (the goalkeeper excepted) shall not intentionally handle the ball. A player shall not use his hands to hold or push an opponent. Charging is permissible, but it must not be violent or dangerous. A player shall not be charged from behind unless he is intentionally obstructing an opponent.

10. When a free-kick has been awarded, the kicker's opponents shall not approach within 6 yards of the ball unless they are standing on their own goal line. The ball at least must be rolled over before it shall be considered played, i.e. it must make a complete circuit or travel the difference of its circumference. The kicker shall not

play the ball a second time until it has been played by another player. The kick-off (except as provided by Law 2), corner kick, and goal kick, shall be free-kicks within the meaning of this Law.

11. A goal may be scored from a free-kick that is awarded because of any infringement of Law 9, but not from any other free-kick.

12. A player shall not wear any nails, except such as have their heads driven in flush with the leather, or metal plates or projections, or gutta-percha on his boots, or on his shin guards. If bars or studs on the soles or heels of the boots are used, they shall not project more than half an inch, and shall have all their fastenings driven in flush with the leather. Bars shall be transverse and flat, not less than half an inch in width, and shall extend from side to side of the boot. Studs shall be round in plan, not less than half an inch in diameter, and in no case conical or pointed. Any player discovered infringing this Law shall be prohibited from taking further part in the match. The Referee shall, if required, examine the players' boots before the commencement of a match.

13. A Referee shall be appointed, whose duties shall be to enforce the Laws and decide all disputed points; and his decision on points of fact connected with the play shall be final. He shall also keep a record of the game, and act as timekeeper. In the event of any ungentlemanly behaviour on the part of any of the players, the offender or offenders shall be cautioned, and if the

offence is repeated, or in case of violent conduct without any previous caution, the Referee shall have power to order the offending player or players off the field of play, and shall transmit the name or names of such player or players to his or their National Association, who shall deal with the matter. The Referee shall have power to allow for time wasted, to suspend the game when he thinks fit, and to terminate the game whenever, by reason of darkness, interference by spectators, or other cause, he may deem necessary; but in all cases in which a game is so terminated he shall report the same to the Association under whose jurisdiction the game was played, who shall have full power to deal with the matter. The Referee shall have power to award a free-kick in any case in which he thinks the conduct of a player dangerous, or likely to prove dangerous, but not sufficiently so as to justify him in putting in force the greater powers vested in him. The power of the Referee extends to offences committed when the play has been temporarily suspended, and when the ball is out of play.

14. Two linesmen shall be appointed, whose duty (subject to the decision of the Referee) shall be to decide when the ball is out of play, and which side is entitled to the corner kick, goal kick, or throw-in; and to assist the Referee in carrying out the game in accordance with the Laws. In the event of any undue interference or improper conduct by a Linesman, the Referee shall

have power to order him off the field of play and appoint a substitute, and report the circumstances to the National Association having jurisdiction over him, who shall deal with the matter.

15. In the event of a supposed infringement of the Laws, the ball shall be in play until a decision has been given.

16. In the event of any temporary suspension of play from any cause, the ball not having gone into touch or behind the goal line, the Referee shall throw the ball down where it was when play was suspended, and it shall be in play when it has touched the ground. If the ball goes into touch or behind the goal line before it is played by a player, the Referee shall again throw it down. The players on either side shall not play the ball until it has touched the ground.

17. In the event of any infringement of Laws 5, 6, 8, 10 or 16, a free-kick shall be awarded to the opposite side, from the place where the infringement occurred. In the event of any intentional infringement of Law 9 outside the penalty area, or by the attacking side within the penalty area, a free-kick shall be awarded to the opposite side from the place where the infringement occurred. In the event of any intentional infringement of Law 9 by the defending side within the penalty area, the Referee shall award the opponents a penalty kick that shall be taken from the penalty kick mark under the following conditions: all players, with the exception of the player taking the penalty kick and the opponents'

goalkeeper, shall be outside the penalty area. The opponents' goalkeeper shall not advance beyond his goal line. The ball must be kicked forward. The ball shall be in play when the kick is taken, and a goal may be scored from a penalty kick; but the ball shall not be again played by the kicker until it has been played by another player. If necessary, time of play shall be extended to admit of the penalty kick being taken. A free-kick shall also be awarded to the opposite side if the ball is not kicked forward, or is played a second time by the player who takes the penalty kick until it has been played by another player. The Referee may refrain from putting the provisions of this Law into effect in cases where he is satisfied that by enforcing them he would be giving an advantage to the offending side. If when a penalty kick is taken the ball passes between the goalposts, under the bar, the goal shall not be nullified by reason of any infringement by the defending side.

## Definition Of Terms

A PLACE KICK is a kick at the ball while it is on the ground in the centre of the field of play.

A FREE-KICK is a kick at the ball in any direction the player pleases, when it is lying on the ground.

A place kick, a free-kick, or a penalty kick must not be taken until the Referee has given a signal for the same.

CARRYING by the goalkeeper is taking more than two steps while holding the ball, or bouncing it on the hand.

KNOCKING ON is when a player strikes or propels the ball with his hands or arms.

HANDLING is intentionally playing the ball with the hand or arm.

TRIPPING is intentionally throwing, or attempting to throw, an opponent by the use of the legs, or by stooping in front of or behind him.

HOLDING includes the obstruction of a player by the hand or any part of the arm extended from the body.

TOUCH is that part of the ground on either side of the field of play.

## The International Football Association Board Rules

1. This Board shall be called the International Football Association Board. The Football Association, the Football Association of Wales, the Scottish Football Association and the Irish Football Association shall each be entitled to send two representatives, who shall constitute the Board.

2. The Board shall discuss and decide proposed alterations in the Laws of the Game, and such matters affecting Association Football in its International relations, as may be referred to them after consideration by either the

governing bodies or General Meetings of the Associations forming the Board.

3. The governing bodies of each Association shall forward in writing, on or before the 1st day of April in each year, to the Secretary of the Association entitled to convene the next meeting, any suggestions or alterations deemed desirable, which shall be printed and distributed on or before the 20th day of April for consideration at the Annual General Meetings of the Associations.

4. The Board shall meet annually on the second Saturday in June, at the invitation of each Association in order of seniority. One of the representatives of the Association convening the meeting shall preside, and the other shall act as Secretary.

5. The Minute Book of the proceedings shall be fully entered up by the Secretary, and forwarded to the Association next in rotation before the 1st of June ensuing.

6. Business shall not be proceeded with at any meeting unless three Associations are represented.

7. No alterations shall be made in the Laws of the Game except at the Annual Meeting in June, and then only on the unanimous vote of the members present. Other resolutions shall not be adopted unless agreed to by three-fourths of those present.

8. The Association, which by order of rotation is entitled to convene the Annual Meeting for the current year, on receiving a written requisition signed by two of the Associations, accompanied by a copy of the proposals

intended to be submitted, shall call a Special Meeting of the Board. Such Special Meeting must be held within twenty-eight days of the receipt of the requisition, and the four Associations forming the Board must receive twenty-one days' notice, together with a copy of the proposals.

9.    The decisions of this Board shall be at once binding on all the Associations, and no alteration in the Laws of the Game made by any Association shall be valid until accepted by this Board.

## Rules Of The Challenge Cup Competition

1.    The Cup shall be called The Football Association Challenge Cup.

2.    The Cup is the property of the Football Association Limited.

3.    The entire control and management of the competition shall be vested in the Council.

4.    The competition shall be open to all Clubs belonging to this or an affiliated Association and approved by the Council. The Cup shall be competed for annually in accordance with these rules by eleven members, who, unless a satisfactory reason is given shall represent the full available strength of each competing Club. The players shall also be duly qualified according to the Rules of the Association.

5.    Each Club desirous of competing shall give notice of such desire to the Secretary of the Association on or before 1st day of May previous to that season in which such

Club proposes to compete, and shall with such notice forward an entrance fee of ten shillings. Clubs (other than the four Clubs that competed in the Semi-final Ties of the previous season) desiring to be exempted in the Qualifying Competition must give notice of such desire and forward the entrance fee before the 20th day of March. An Amateur Club competing for this Cup may also compete for the Amateur Challenge Cup. The Council may reject the entry of any Club if they deem such a course desirable.

6.   A player shall not in the same season play for more than one competing Club, but the members of each respective team may be changed during the series of matches. In the preliminary and the first and second rounds of the Qualifying Competition, it is not necessary for a player to possess any other qualification than that required by the rules of the Association. Except in the preliminary and the first and second rounds of the Qualifying Competition, a player must have been a recognised playing member of his Club for at least fourteen days previous to the date fixed for playing the match. A playing member is one who has either actually played for his Club in the current season, or who has, in writing, intimated to the Secretary of the Association that he is a playing member of that Club. The Secretary shall, in writing, acknowledge the receipt of every such intimation. A player qualified to play in any round, shall be deemed qualified to play in any subsequent round by virtue

of his original qualification. In the case of postponed, drawn or replayed matches, only those players shall be allowed to play who were eligible on the date fixed for the completion of the round in which the match was originally played.

7.  Every Club playing in the Competition proper shall, not less than five days before the match, send to the opposing Club a list of players from which the team for such match will be selected; and no objection to the qualification of any player mentioned in such list shall be entertained, unless notice of objection, stating particulars, is given at least twenty-four hours before the commencement of the match. In the case of a postponed, drawn or replayed match, the above periods of time shall be observed so far as circumstances will permit. Lists and objections must be sent by registered letter.

8.  If the Council have any doubt as to the qualification of any player taking part in this competition, they shall have power to call upon such player, or the Club to which he belongs, or for which he played, to prove that he is qualified according to the Rules, and failing satisfactory proof the Council may disqualify such player, and may remove the Club from the competition, or impose such other penalty as they may think fit. Any Club making a frivolous objection will be liable to removal from the Competition.

9.  The Council shall have the power to disqualify any competing Club, or player,

or players for any competing Club, who may be proved to be guilty of any breach of the Rules of the Association.

10. There shall be a Qualifying Competition, and a Competition Proper.

    The four Clubs that competed in the Semi-Final Ties of the previous season, and (provided they have again entered) forty-eight Clubs to be selected by the Council from those that competed in the previous season shall be exempted till the Competition Proper. Notice shall be given of the date upon which such selection will be made, but application must be made for exemption before the 20th day of March, according to Rule 5.

11. The Qualifying Competition shall consist of all other Clubs. Of these twelve Clubs shall be selected by the Council from those that competed in the previous season (provided they have again entered), and these shall be exempted until the last round of the Qualifying Competition. The other Clubs shall be divided into twenty-four Divisions geographically convenient and as nearly equal in number of Clubs as possible, and these shall compete until only one is left in each Division. The winners in the twenty-four Divisions shall be divided into twelve Divisions geographically convenient, and these shall play one round. The twelve Clubs selected under this rule and the winners of the twelve Divisions shall then be drawn together and compete in the last round of the Qualifying Competition. The winners of this round

shall compete in the Competition Proper. All necessary byes shall be given in the first round of the Qualifying Competition, and the Competition shall be completed on or before the 22nd day of December. The Qualifying Competition (except the last round) shall be managed by Divisional Committees appointed by the Council, whose decisions shall be final, and whose powers for managing the Competition shall be the same as those of the Council.

12.  The Competition Proper shall consist of the fifty-two Clubs that are exempted from the Qualifying Competition and the twelve winners of the Qualifying Competition. These shall compete until the Final Tie is played, when the winning Club shall hold the Cup for the current year.

13.  The Clubs, after being placed by the Council in the proper Competitions, shall be drawn in couples. These couples shall compete, and the winners shall be drawn and shall compete in the same manner, and this shall be continued until the end of the Competition. Immediately after each draw is made, notice shall be given to each Club of the name of its opponent, and the date and hour when the tie shall be played. All ties in each round shall be played on one date and at such hours as the Council may determine.

14.  Unless otherwise mutually arranged, the Club that is in each instance first drawn in the ballot shall have choice of ground. Except as provided by Rule 29, a Club shall not be allowed to select a ground other than that on which it is accustomed

to play without the consent of the opposing Club. In the case of replayed matches, the Club that did not have the choice of ground for the first match shall have the choice of ground for the second match. If the ground of the Club having choice of ground is considered unsuitable for a Cup Tie, the opposing club may appeal to the Council within three days of the receipt of the official intimation of the draw. Such appeal must be accompanied by a fee of two guineas, which shall be forfeited if the appeal is not sustained. The Council may order the match to be played on the ground of the appealing Club, or on a neutral ground. If such appeal be not sustained, the complaining Club may be called upon to pay the expenses incurred in deciding the appeal. Each Club must take every precaution to keep its ground in playing condition, and if necessary, either Club may require the referee to visit the ground two hours before the advertised time to kick off, and decide as to its fitness for play. Clubs shall not mutually arrange to play a match in lieu of a Cup Tie. If a match is played to a conclusion, it must be a Cup Tie, but if from any cause a match is not completed, it must be replayed the full time of one hour and a half. Postponed matches shall be played on the following Saturday, unless the Clubs agree to an earlier date. This Rule does not apply to Semi-final and Final Ties.

15. The duration of each match shall be one hour and a half, and the referee shall allow

for time wasted or lost through accident or other cause.

16. In all matches preceding the Semi-final Ties the following provisions shall apply. An extra half-hour may be played in matches that result in a draw, provided the two Clubs mutually agree and intimate their decision to the referee before the match commences. When a match has resulted in a draw, it must be replayed on the following Thursday, unless the Clubs mutually agree at the conclusion of the match to an earlier day, and at once jointly intimate their decision to the Secretary of the Association. If the second match should also result in a draw, it must be replayed not later than the following Monday, and the Council shall fix the ground and day, unless the Clubs mutually agree at the conclusion of the match and at once jointly intimate their decision to the Secretary of the Association. When a replayed match has resulted in a draw, an extra half hour must be played.

17. Any Club intending to scratch must give information of their intention to do so to the Secretary of the opposing Club not less than eight days before the date fixed for playing. A Club failing to comply with this rule shall be reported to the Council, who shall have power to compel such offending Club to pay the expenses incurred by their opponents, or of taking such action as they may deem expedient. If a Club decides to scratch after a drawn game, intimation must be given to its opponent at the close of the match.

18.  The Council shall fix the grounds for all Semi-final and Final Ties, and shall have direct control of all the arrangements connected with these matches. When a Semi-final match has resulted in a draw, it must be replayed on the following Thursday, unless the Clubs mutually agree at the conclusion of the match to play on the Wednesday, and at once jointly intimate their decision to the Secretary of the Association. If the second match should also result in a draw, it must be replayed on the following Monday, unless the Clubs mutually agree at the conclusion of the match to play on an earlier day, and at once jointly intimate their decision to the Secretary of the Association. When a final match has resulted in a draw it must be replayed on or before the following Saturday, as the Council may determine. If the second match should also result in a draw, it must be replayed on or before the following Thursday, as the Council may determine. When a replayed match under this Rule has resulted in a draw an extra half-hour must be played.

19.  In the Semi-final and Final Ties any Club failing to play, without showing a good and sufficient cause for such failure to play, may be adjudged by the Council to have been guilty of serious misconduct, and liable to be dealt with under Rule 45 of the Association.

20.  The dimensions of the field of play for Cup Ties shall be as follows: for Semi-final and Final Ties, 115 yards by 70 to 75

yards. For all other ties, maximum length, 120 yards; minimum length, 110 yards; maximum breadth, 80 yards; minimum breadth, 70 yards. Goal nets must be used in all ties.

21. In the Qualifying Competition (except the last round thereof), Referees shall be appointed by the Divisional Committees, and the Clubs may appoint Linesmen. In the last round of the Qualifying Competition, and in the Competition Proper, the Council shall appoint the Referees and Linesmen, and neither past nor present members of the contending Clubs shall be eligible. The expenses of all officials appointed by the Council to officiate in any match prior to the Semi-final and Final Ties shall be paid by the Club upon whose ground the match takes place.

22. The Referee shall have power to decide as to the fitness of the ground in all matches, and in other respects the duties of the Referee and Linesman shall be as defined in Laws of the Game 13 and 14.

23. The Secretary of the winning Club, or in case of a draw the Secretary of each Club, shall send notice of the result, in writing, to the Secretary of the Association within two days after the match is played (Sundays not included). Clubs failing to comply with this rule shall be subject to a fine of 10s, and in default of payment shall be struck out of the competition.

24. All questions relating to the qualification of competitors, or interpretation of the Rules, or any dispute or protest whatever,

shall be referred to the Council, whose decision shall be final and binding on both Clubs. Every protest must be made in writing, and must contain the particulars of the grounds upon which it is founded. Two copies of the protest must be lodged with the Association, accompanied by a fee of two guineas, within two days of the match to which it relates (Sundays not included). The fee shall be forfeited to the Association in the event of the protest not being sustained. The Council may order any Club engaged in a dispute or protest to pay such sum as may be considered necessary towards defraying the expenses incurred. Any protest relating to the ground, goalposts or bars, or other appurtenances of the game, shall not be entertained by the Council unless an objection has been lodged with the Referee before the commencement of the match. The Referee shall require the responsible Club to remove the cause of objection, if this is possible without unduly delaying the progress of the match. When an objection has been lodged with the Referee, a protest must be made to the Association, and neither objection nor protest shall be withdrawn, except by leave of the Council.

25. The Secretary of the Association shall send a copy of the protest and particulars to the Club protested against. Each Club may support its case by witnesses. If a member of the Council is connected with a Club concerned in a dispute or protest, he shall

not sit on the Council while the dispute or protest is being considered. Neither Barrister nor Solicitor shall represent a Club at the hearing of a dispute or protest, unless he be the Secretary of the Club concerned, and appear as such in the printed list of Secretaries in the Official Rule Book.

26. The proceeds of matches (except replayed matches in consequence of breach of Rule) shall, after paying thereout the advertising, ground and other expenses of the match, and third-class railway fares of the eleven players of the visiting Club, be divided as follows:

(1) In a match prior to the Competition Proper, equally between the Competing Clubs.

(2) In a match in the Competition Proper (except Semi-final and Final Ties), five per cent, of the gross gates shall be paid to the Association, and the balance equally divided between the Competing Clubs.

(3) In Semi-final and Final Ties, as provided by Rule 30. If the receipts are not sufficient to cover the entire expenses of the match, the advertising, ground and other expenses (except railway fares), shall be a first charge. The home Club shall provide for the sale of tickets, and the visiting Club for checking the sale. The expenses of

sellers and checkers shall not be a charge on the gate. All members or ticket holders shall pay the admission charges to the ground and stands. The gate receipts shall be approximately divided immediately after the match, and a full statement and settlement shall be made within seven days of the match.

27. When a match is postponed through causes over which neither Club has any control, the expenses shall be paid out of the receipts of the second match.

28. In any match ordered to be replayed in consequence of a breach of Rule, the Club in default shall not receive any share of the proceeds of such replayed match (except third-class railway fares for the eleven players) without the consent of the Council, and such consent shall only be given under special circumstances. If consent be not given, the share shall be taken by the Association.

29. A Club not having a private ground shall provide a private or enclosed ground, where gate money shall be charged for Cup Ties, free of all charge to the visiting Club, or play on its opponent's ground.

30. The Council shall, at the end of each year, ascertain the balance in favour of the General Account (as provided for by Rule 19 of the Association), and shall divide such balance among the Clubs competing in the Semi-final and Final Ties pro rata as

to the net gate receipts of each particular tie, provided always, that the sum to be so divided shall not in any case exceed the total sum of the net gate receipts of the Semi-final and Final Ties.

31. When the winning Club has been ascertained, the Association shall deliver the Cup to such Club, which shall be responsible for its return to the Treasurer of the Association on or before the 1st day of February in the ensuing year, in good order and condition. Should the Cup be destroyed or damaged by fire or other accident while under the care or custody of the Club, the Club shall refund to the Association the amount of its original value or the cost of thorough repair, and should the Cup be lost or destroyed from any other cause while under the care or custody of the Club, the Club shall in addition to any other penalty that the Association may impose, pay to the Association a sum of £100 for liquidated damages.

32. In addition to the Cup, the Association shall present Medals or Badges to the players in the Final Tie.

33. All notices required to be given to the Association by any of these Rules shall be addressed to the Secretary, at the offices of The Football Association Ltd, 104, High Holborn, London, W.C.

34. The Council shall have power to alter or add to the above Rules as they from time to time deem expedient

## Rules of the Amateur Challenge Cup Competition

1. The Cup shall be called The Football Association Amateur Challenge Cup.
2. The Cup is the property of the Football Association Limited.
3. The entire control and management of the Competition shall be vested in the Council.
4. The Competition shall be open to all amateur Clubs belonging to this or an affiliated Association and approved by the Council. The Cup shall be competed for annually in accordance with the following rules by eleven members (amateurs), who, unless a satisfactory reason is given, shall represent the full available strength of each competing Club. Any Club having one or more professionals registered is not an Amateur Club within the meaning of this Rule.
5. A professional who has been reinstated as an amateur after 1902 shall not be eligible to play in this Competition.
6. Each Club desirous of competing shall give notice of such desire to the Secretary of the Association, on or before the 1st day of September previous to that season in which such Club proposes to compete, and shall with such notice forward an entrance fee of ten shillings. The Council may reject the entry of any Club if they deem such a course desirable. Clubs desiring to be excused the Qualifying Competition under Rule 11 must give notice of such desire,

and forward their entrance fees before the 15th day of May in each year.

7.  A member shall not be allowed to play for more than one competing club, but the players of each representative team may be changed during the series of matches. In the Qualifying Competition, each player must have been a playing member of the Club for which he proposes to compete at least twenty-eight days previous to the day fixed for playing the match, except as hereinafter provided. In the first round of the Qualifying Competition, no such twenty-eight days qualification is required, and in the second round, when it is fixed to be played within twenty-eight days from the date fixed for the first round, each player must have been a playing member of the Club for which he proposes to compete at least fourteen days previous to the day fixed for playing the match. For the purposes of the Qualifying Competition, a playing member of a Club is one who has either actually played for the Club during the current or the previous Season, or one who has since the previous Season in writing intimated to the Secretary of the Association that he is a playing member of that Club. The Secretary of the Association shall, in writing, acknowledge the receipt of every such intimation. In the Competition proper, each player must have played twice for his Club in the current season at least twenty-eight days previous to the day fixed for playing the match. In the case of postponed, drawn or

replayed matches, only those players shall be allowed to play who were eligible on the date fixed for the completion of the round in which the match was originally played. The twenty-eight and fourteen days qualifications are not required for a player playing with a Club consisting of old boys of any one Public School. Such Public School player shall also be eligible to play in the Competition Proper, although he may not have played twice for his Club in the current season.

8.    If the Council have any doubt as to the qualification of any player taking part in this competition, they shall have power to call upon such player, or the Club to which he belongs, or for which he played, to prove that he is qualified according to the Rules, and failing satisfactory proof the Council may disqualify such player, and may remove the Club from the Competition, or impose such other penalty as they may think fit.

9.    The Council shall have the power to disqualify any competing Club, or player, or players for any competing Club who may be proved to be guilty of any breach of the Rules of the Association.

10.   The Council shall divide the competing Clubs into two Divisions, viz. the Northern Division and the Southern Division, and in each of these two Divisions there shall be a Qualifying Competition and a Competition Proper.

11.   The Competition shall be conducted in the following manner:

In each Division, ten Clubs (including the two last Clubs left in the Division in the previous year's Competition, provided they have complied with Rule 6) shall be excused the Qualifying Competition.

The Clubs not so excused in each Division shall be divided into six Districts geographically convenient, and shall compete in a Qualifying Competition until only one Club is left in each of the six Districts. The Council shall have the power to divide each District into groups if thought necessary.

All Clubs, including the two last Clubs left in each Division, desiring to be excused, shall give notice before the 15th day of May in each year, according to Rule 6.

12. The Qualifying Competitions shall be completed by 31 December. All the necessary byes shall be given in the Qualifying Competitions, and all the Ties in each round shall be played on one date and at such hours as the Council may determine.

13. The Clubs excused the Qualifying Competitions, together with the District winners in each Division, shall enter the Competition Proper. The Clubs in the Competition Proper of each Division shall then be subdivided into groups at the discretion of the Council and drawn in couples and shall compete among themselves until one Club is left. The winner of the Northern Division shall meet the winner of the Southern Division

in the Final Tie, and the winning Club shall hold the Cup for the current year.

14. The Secretary of the Association shall, immediately after each draw is made, intimate to each Club the name of its opponent and the date and hour when the Tie shall be played.

15. Unless otherwise mutually arranged, the Club that is in each instance first drawn in the ballot shall have choice of ground. Except as provided by Rule 31, a Club shall not be allowed to select a ground other than that on which it is accustomed to play, without the consent of the opposing Club. In the case of replayed matches, the Club that did not have the choice of ground for the first match shall have choice of ground for the second match. If the ground of the Club having choice of ground is considered unsuitable for a Cup Tie, the opposing Club may appeal to the Council within three days of the receipt of the official intimation of the draw. The Council may order the match to be played on the ground of the appealing Club, or on a neutral ground. If such appeal be not sustained, the complaining Club may be called upon to pay the expenses incurred in deciding the appeal. Each club must take every precaution to keep its ground in playing condition, and if necessary, either Club may apply to the Association, and the Secretary shall require the Referee or some other person to examine the ground and decide as to its fitness for play in sufficient time to save expenses being incurred by

the Clubs of unnecessary journeys. Clubs shall not mutually arrange to play a match in lieu of a Cup Tie. If a match is played to a conclusion, it must be a Cup Tie, but if from any cause a match is not completed it must be replayed the full time of one hour and a half. Postponed matches shall be played on the following Saturday, unless the Clubs agree to an earlier date. This Rule does not apply to the last match in each Division (which matches shall be considered the Semi-final Ties) and to the Final Tie.

16. The duration of each match shall be one hour and a half, and the Referee shall allow for time wasted or lost through accident or other cause.

17. In all matches preceding the Semi-final Ties, the following provisions shall apply. An extra half-hour may be played in matches that result in a draw, provided the two Clubs mutually agree and intimate their decision to the Referee before the match commences. When a match has resulted in a draw it must be replayed on the following Saturday, unless the Clubs mutually agree at the conclusion of the match to an earlier day, and at once jointly intimate their decision to the Secretary of the Association. If the second match should also result in a draw it must be replayed not later than the following Wednesday, and the Council shall fix the ground and day unless the Clubs mutually agree at the conclusion of the match, and at once jointly intimate their decision to

the Secretary of the Association. When a replayed match has resulted in a draw, an extra half-hour must be played.

18. Any Club intending to scratch must give information of their intention to do so to the Secretary of the opposing Club not less than eight days before the date fixed for playing. A Club failing to comply with this Rule shall be reported to the Council, who shall have power to compel such offending Club to pay the expenses incurred by their opponents, or of taking such action as they may deem expedient.

19. The Council shall fix the grounds for all Semi-final and Final Ties, and shall have direct control of all the arrangements connected with these matches. When a Semi-final match has resulted in a draw, it must be replayed on the following Saturday. If the second match should also result in a draw, it must be replayed on the following Thursday, unless the Clubs mutually agree at the conclusion of the match to play on an earlier day, and at once jointly intimate their decision to the Secretary of the Association. When a Final match has resulted in a draw, it must be replayed on the following Saturday. If the second match should also result in a draw, it must be replayed as the Council may determine. When a replayed match under this Rule has resulted in a draw, an extra half-hour must be played.

20. In the Semi-final and Final Ties any Club failing to play, without showing a good and sufficient cause for such failure to play, may be

adjudged by the Council to have been guilty of serious misconduct, and liable to be dealt with under Rule 45 of the Association.

21.  The dimensions of the field of play for Cup Ties shall be: maximum length, 120 yards; minimum length, 110 yards; maximum breadth, 80 yards; minimum breadth, 70 yards. Goal nets must be used in all ties in the Competition Proper, and the Council recommend their use in the Qualifying Competition.

22.  The Referee in all matches shall be neither a past nor present member of either of the contending Clubs. The fees and travelling expenses of all officials appointed by the Council to officiate in any match prior to the Semi-final and Final Ties shall be paid by the Club upon whose ground the match takes place. Subject to Rule 15, the Referee shall have power to decide as to the fitness of the ground in all matches, and in other respects the duties of the Referee and Linesmen shall be as defined in Laws of the Game 13 and 14.

23.  In the Qualifying Competition, the competing Clubs may agree upon a Referee, in which case either side must notify such appointment to the Secretary of the Association. If, however, they should be unable to agree upon a Referee, they shall apply to the Secretary, who shall appoint one, such application to be made seven days before the day of the match. Each Club may appoint a Linesman.

24.  The Council shall appoint the Referees in the Competition Proper, and Linesmen

in the Semi-final and Final Ties. In the Competition Proper, previous to the Semi-final Ties, Clubs may agree upon neutral Linesmen. If, however, they should be unable to agree upon Linesmen, they shall apply to the Secretary, who shall appoint them, such applications to be made seven days before the day of the match.

25.  The Secretary of the winning Club, or in the case of a draw the Secretary of each Club, shall send notice of the result, in writing, to the Secretary of the Association within two days after the match (Sundays not included). Clubs failing to comply with this Rule shall be subject to a fine of 10s, and in default of payment shall be struck out of the competition.

26.  All questions relating to the qualification of competitors, or interpretation of the Rules, or any dispute or protest whatever, shall be referred to the Council, whose decision shall be final and binding on both Clubs. Every protest must be made in writing, and must contain the particulars of the grounds upon which it is founded. Two copies of the protest must be lodged with the Association, accompanied by a fee of two guineas, within two days of the match to which it relates (Sundays not included). The fee shall be forfeited to the Association in the event of the protest not being sustained. The Council may order any Club engaged in a dispute or protest to pay such sum as may be considered necessary towards defraying

the expenses incurred. Any protest relating to the ground, goalposts, or bars, or other appurtenances of the game, shall not be entertained by the Council, unless an objection has been lodged with the Referee before the commencement of the match. The Referee shall require the responsible Club to remove the cause of objection, if this is possible without unduly delaying the progress of the match. When an objection has been lodged with the Referee, a protest must be made to the Association, and no objection or protest shall be withdrawn except by leave of the Council.

27.  The Secretary of the Association shall send a copy of the protest and particulars to the Club protested against. Each Club may support its case by witnesses. If a member of the Council is connected with a Club concerned in a dispute or protest, he shall not sit on the Council while the dispute or protest is being considered. Neither Barrister nor Solicitor shall represent a Club at the hearing of a dispute or protest, unless he be the Secretary of the Club concerned, and appear as such in the printed list of Secretaries in the Official Rule Book.

28.  The proceeds of matches (except replayed matches in consequence of a breach of Rule, and Semi-final and Final Ties) shall be equally divided between the competing Clubs, after paying thereout the advertising, ground and other expenses of the match, and third-class railway fares of the eleven players of the visiting

Club. In cases where the receipts are not sufficient to cover the entire expenses of the match, the fees and travelling expenses of the officials shall be a first charge upon the receipts, after payment of which the residue of the receipts shall be applied pro rata in payment of the railway fares of the visiting team and the ground and other expenses.

The home Club shall provide for the sale of tickets, and the visiting Club for checking the sale. The expenses of sellers and checkers shall not be a charge on the gate. All members or ticket holders shall pay the admission charges to the ground and stands. The gate receipts shall be approximately divided immediately after the match, and a full statement and settlement shall be made within seven days of the match. Clubs that, in the Qualifying Competition, do not charge for admission to their ground shall not be entitled to a share of the admission charges of other Clubs in replayed matches.

29. When a match is postponed through causes over which neither Club has any control, the expenses shall be paid out of the receipts of the second match.

30. In any match ordered to be replayed in consequence of a breach of Rule, the Club in default shall not receive any share of the proceeds of such replayed match (except third-class railway fares for the eleven players) without the consent of the Council, and such consent shall only be given under special circumstances. If

consent is not given, the share shall be taken by the Association.

31.  A Club not having a private or enclosed ground shall provide one, free of all charge, to the visiting Club, or play on its opponent's ground. In the Competition proper, gate money must be charged.

32.  The Council shall, at the end of each year, ascertain the balance in favour of the General Account (as provided by Rule 19 of the Association), and shall divide such balance among the Clubs competing in the Semi-final and Final Ties pro rata as to the net gate receipts of each particular Tie, provided always, that the sum to be so divided shall not in any case exceed the total sum of the net gate receipts of the Semi-final and Final Ties.

33.  When the winning Club shall have been ascertained, the Association shall deliver the Cup to such Club, which shall be responsible for its return to the Treasurer of the Association on or before the 1st day of February in the ensuing year, in good order and condition. Should the Cup be destroyed or damaged by fire or other accident while under the care or custody of the Club, the Club shall refund to the Association the amount of its original value or the cost of thorough repair. Should the Cup be lost or destroyed from any other cause while under the care or custody of the Club, the Club shall, in addition to any other penalty that the Association may impose, pay to the Association a sum of £100 as and for liquidated damages.

34.   In addition to the Cup, the Association shall present Medals or Badges to the players in the Final Tie.

35.   All notices required to be given to the Association by any of these Rules shall be addressed to the Secretary, at the offices of The Football Association Limited, 104, High Holborn, London, W.C.

36.   The Council shall have power to alter or add to the above Rules as they from time to time deem expedient.